LEADER

STEAM'S LAST CHANCE

LEADER
STEAM'S LAST CHANCE
KEVIN ROBERTSON

ALAN SUTTON

1988

ALAN SUTTON PUBLISHING
BRUNSWICK ROAD · GLOUCESTER

First published 1988

British Library Cataloguing in Publication Data

Robertson, Kevin
Leader : steam's last chance.
1. Bulleid, O.V.S.   2. Southern Railway
Company—History   3. Locomotives—
England—Design and construction
I. Title
625.2'61'0924   TJ140.B78

ISBN 0-86299-376-8

*Front Cover: 'Leader' – What might have been. From a painting by Mike Turner, reproduced
by permission of Les Warnett.
Front Flap: No. 36001 at Eastleigh in June 1949 – S.C. Townroe.
Endpapers: 'Leader' and dynamometer car test train at Allbrook just north of Eastleigh –
S.C. Townroe.*

Typesetting and origination by
Alan Sutton Publishing Limited
Printed in Great Britain

For Les Warnett

ACKNOWLEDGEMENTS

It was with little serious consideration that I first became involved in the research of the 'Leader' concept. But as time progressed and the whole story began to unravel it became clear that not only was an enormous amount of work involved, but also a considerable requirement in time. In order to present an objective viewpoint within the book I have attempted to judge 'Leader' from a number of distinct angles; historical, political, engineering, operating and traffic and I am grateful to all those sited below who have so willingly assisted in one or more of these categories.

Foremost amongst the credits are three individuals, Les Warnett who so willingly provided a technical description, as well as placing at my disposal a wealth of other material and knowledge based upon his own experience. Stephen Townroe, the former Motive Power Superintendant at Eastleigh in the days of 'Leader', who from this position and engineering knowledge has been an invaluable guide and mentor to the project. And finally Don Broughton for so willingly making available his unique collection of photographs – I well recall a most enjoyable evening in Bournemouth . . . !

I would also like to thank the following, in alphabetical order, space I regret precludes a full acknowledgement of each individual contribution.

Hugh and Joan Abbinnett – sincere thanks as always, H.W. Attwell – whose memories have been invaluable, John Bell, Eric Best – for a most colourful description, sorry it could not be exactly included!, W. Bishop, C.P. Boocock, D.L. Bradley, E. Bramble, P. Bramble, E. Branch, H.A.P. Browne, H.A.V. Bulleid (with grateful thanks for permission to quote from his own book), D. Callender, H.C. Casserley, Derek Clayton (as always), Barry and Joe Curl – for much encouragement, Brian Davis, W. Durban, Les Elsey, John Fairman (one of life's true gentlemen), John Fry – a sincere thank you for everything, Ted Forder, Harry Frith, Geoff Gardiner, Jack Gardner, W. Gilburt, David Fereday Glenn, Roger Hardingham, Graham Hawkins, C.C.B. Herbert, Dave Heulin, Bill Jackson, Phil Kelley, Graham Long, The Institute of Mechanical Engineers and especially S.G. Morrison, Ron Manley and Max Millard – for encouragement and valued help, Tony Molyneaux, B. Musgrave, The National Newspaper Library, The National Railway Museum and especially Phil Atkins and John Edgington without whose help none of this would have been possible, G.L. Nicholson – a most valuable contribution, The Patents Office, Reg Randell – and I thought I was a hoarder!, R.C. Riley – for much patience and a genuine guiding influence – thank you, John Rooney, Reg Roude, The Science Museum, Ian Shawyer (a valued friend), R.C. Simmonds, Roger Simmonds, Alf Smith, Mrs Talbot (for the loan of her precious photographs), Dennis Tillman, *The Times* Photographic Library, J.T. Howard Turner, Fred Waller, George Wheeler, D.W. Winkworth – for much patience, Les Wright and Doug Yarney.

Also in this section a special thanks to Lyn, Jennie, Carole and Sharon, they have had to put up with an awful lot!

Finally I would also like to thank Peter, Lyn and Joyce from Alan Sutton. Their encouragement and guidance is ever visible in the text.

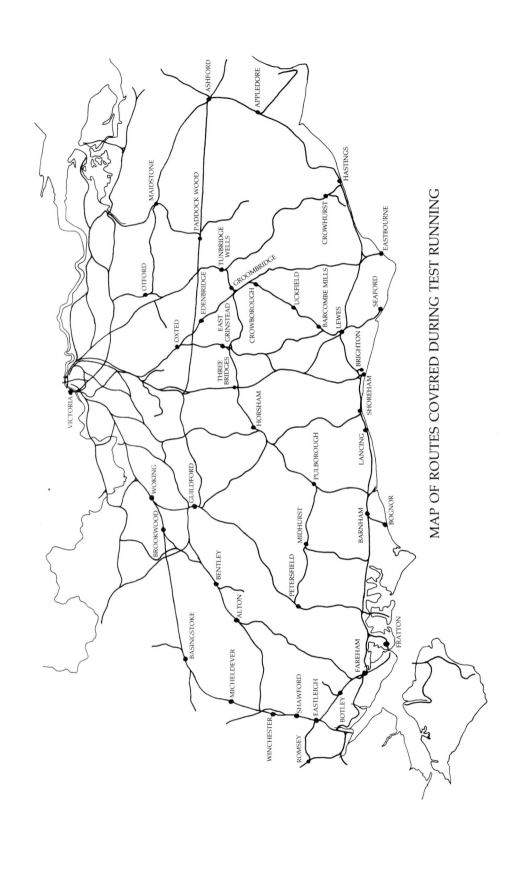

MAP OF ROUTES COVERED DURING TEST RUNNING

CONTENTS

'Leader', arguably the ultimate in steam locomotive design, certainly the most controversial. Was this the way forward? Apart from the exhaust, one could be forgiven for thinking this was no steam engine at all, showing little resemblance to anything previously seen.

Times Newspapers Ltd

FOREWORD

The author has a lifelong interest in railways and is married to a railwayman's daughter. Originally, to keep active during a period of illness, he started to gather evidence for a book on a type of experimental steam locomotive about which little had, or has since, been published.

To unravel events that happened over 35 years ago has required the perseverence of a detective and the interviewing of such elderly witnesses as could be found with first-hand knowledge. The result is a record as reliable as possible. Some documentary evidence has survived, thanks to the existence of a National Railway Museum.

Kevin Robertson has succeeded in establishing a narrative of the building and testing of the 'Leader' class locomotive beyond reasonable doubt, but the reasoning behind much of the design details, so many of them faulty, must ever remain inexplicable. You might call the book not a Whodunit but a Whydunit!

Stephen Townroe

PREFACE

Twenty years ago, the prolific railway writer, O.S. Nock, when commenting on 'Leader' said, 'I feel it is still too early to give a reasonable appraisal of an experiment which can only be described as fully in keeping with the personality and career of the designer'.

Two decades later I feel that the time may now be right, although it has become very obvious to me that there are many who still hold strong feelings either for or against the whole 'Leader' concept.

Accordingly, it has at times, been very difficult to adopt an un-biased attitude towards the engine. Previous publications have tended to deal only in the outline facts with little space devoted to the eccentricities and charisma of the machine itself. This is certainly not the fault of the writers concerned, as faced with a limited amount of space it is difficult to devote sufficient coverage to what was indeed only a part of Bulleid's life.

In attempting to present the full story of 'Leader' I have tried to present the evidence both for and against the project with, wherever possible, important corroboration. If the information has not been to hand then I have drawn my own conclusions. I have indicated these when mentioned as such in the text and I make no excuses if any of my conclusions are in any way controversial, based as they are upon the results of research.

With the bulk of official records tending to condemn the project there is a temptation to immediately dismiss 'Leader'. However to do so is to adopt a narrow minded attitude as the concept must be viewed as a whole.

I submit then my own personal efforts at recording the events appertaining to Leader, both factual and political, between the period 1945 to 1951. The anticipation, fervour and eventual defeat of this unique machine. A final challenge by steam against the diesel.

Kevin Robertson

21 JUNE 1949

To the holidaymakers of Brighton who awoke to a bright summer morning there was the promise of a fine day ahead. A day which would perhaps be spent building sandcastles or walking along the promenade and pier before returning to lunch at one of the numerous sea-front hotels and guesthouses. Any idea of work to be cast to the back of the mind, a melancholy thought banished during this the annual family holiday.

No. 36001, the first and only 'Leader' to be completed, shown alongside the main line at Brighton, 21 June 1949.

H.M. Madgwick

Who then amongst the visitors to the town on that June day realised that a matter of a mile or so from the sea-front history was being made? For on that same morning a remarkable steam engine was slowly pulled out of the locomotive workshops alongside the station to stand by the main line for all to see. 'What is that . . . ?,' one passenger was heard to murmur as his electric train slowed for the final approach to Brighton station. 'Is it one of those new diesel or electric engines . . .?' No, this was 'Leader', a steam design so revolutionary that it bore little resemblance to anything ever seen on the rails of Britain. A steam design that had been five years in development but was destined to survive less than one third of this time once out on the rails.

Despite such a short lifespan the 'Leader' story remains one of the most talked about aspects of the early years of the nationalised railway network. This is due in no small way to the project being within the living memory of many who were intimately involved, and who perhaps retain particularly strong feelings one way or the other.

Accordingly a certain folklore has arisen over 'Leader' and this is not helped by the lack of available official information under the '30 year rule'.

Why then was 'Leader' so different, why indeed was it built in the first place, and why so much controversy? These along with a number of other questions are what the following pages attempt to explain. How one man's search for the ultimate design resulted in the ultimate failure. But was it really a failure, or was it failed? That has been the outstanding question for over thirty years, now perhaps at last the reader may be able to decide.

AN ENGINEER'S DREAM

In 1907 there emerged from the Derby locomotive works of the Midland Railway a privately sponsored 2-6-2 tender engine of a unique design. This was the Paget engine and it predated a number of the principles later included in 'Leader'. (The Paget design is briefly described in Appendix A.)

After a number of trial runs Paget's engine disappeared from sight and was eventually broken up. For many years afterwards little, if any, information was available on the design, until less than four years before 'Leader' first took to the rails the *Railway Gazette* produced a booklet on the engine which contained the following statement;

> 'The inevitable question that confronts one after reading Mr. Clayton's most valuable article, is "Could this engine, with certain modifications, have been made to justify the high hopes placed in her by her designer?" The evidence, scanty though it is, seems to point to an affirmative answer.'

Could the same principles apply to 'Leader'? Time would tell.

Oliver Vaughan Snell Bulleid was born in Invarcargill, New Zealand on 19 September 1882, the first child of William and Marianne Bulleid, emigres from Britain who had arrived in the colony four years previously.

During his lifetime 'O.V.B.' as he became known, was to develop a deserved reputation as an outstanding mechanical engineer. First with the Great Northern Railway and then from 1923–37 as assistant to Nigel (later Sir Nigel) Gresley, Chief Mechanical Engineer of the LNER. However, despite his undoubted talent, Bulleid was at that time little known outside railway and engineering circles. Indeed it seemed as if Gresley kept his assistant well under restraint, for whilst Bulleid's involvement with rolling stock design is well known, there is no record that any of Gresley's locomotives owed much to the Bulleid influence.

That is not to say that these early years were wasted, for Bulleid amassed a wealth of knowledge in both practical as well as workshop practice. Indeed certain of these experiences were to come to the fore after taking over as C.M.E. of the Southern, in particular the use of welding.

Other ideas may well also have had their origins around this time. Was, the decision to offset the boiler on 'Leader', for example, taken from the corridor design of tender used on some of the LNER Pacifics? – certainly they never appeared to suffer from difficulties caused by such unbalanced weight distribution. (In the corridor tenders the inclusion of a narrow passage along one side allowed for the exchange of locomotive crews en route. As a result of this the 6000 gallons of water carried was not equally distributed on either side of the centre line. Weights were carried on the corridor side to effect an acceptable balance.)

It was not until 1937, at the relatively late age of 55, that Bulleid took over as C.M.E. of the Southern Railway and, understandably, wished to display his ideas in practice at the earliest opportunity. This first manifested itself in the design of a buffet car for the 13

3

'4-BUF' electric sets brought out in 1938 for the newly electrified lines in Sussex. Externally the sets were similar to the earlier '4-COR' units, often referred to as 'Nelsons', but inside the new vehicles were arranged with separate bar and saloon sections, with the tables having concave curves in a contemporary styling. A few years later his designs for carriage stock included the double deck trains, modern locomotive hauled coaches and a range of new suburban units.

'O.V.B.'   Collection of B. Curl

However it is for his locomotives that Bulleid is perhaps best remembered. His Pacifics, in their original form, capable of outstanding performance, yet not adverse to lapses of seemingly eccentric behaviour. Perhaps a fitting description of their designer as well.

Bulleid's last steam design for the Southern was officially known as the 'Leader' class and was in effect the culmination of a lifetime of ideas. It was a valiant attempt to depart from the conventional layout of a steam engine and so produce a machine which would have many of the advantages of the diesel and electric engines but still use home produced fuel. This does not mean that he saw no use for the more modern types of motive power, for he was actively involved in the building of main line diesel locomotives for the SR during which time 'Leader' was at the design stage. It is more likely that he developed a wish, some say perhaps unkindly an obsession, to prove the steam engine could match anything more modern and so score with regard to cheaper construction and running costs when compared with the diesels and electrics. All this was of course at a time when coal was still the principle fuel of the nation and oil had to be imported.

This then was the embryo from which 'Leader' grew, and which was to develop into a race against time as the threat of nationalisation advanced. It is still not clear, more than 40 years later how much this race affected the final design. Or how different the finished engine was from that perhaps originally envisaged. Also how much was based on the Paget machine of 40 years earlier? What is almost certain is that the final engine could best be described as a mutant.

Typical of Bulleid was this early 1940s experiment which was intended to disperse exhaust steam more rapidly than a conventional single chimney. The purpose was to reduce the likelihood of an enemy aircraft being able to locate a train by its exhaust. 'King Arthur' class engine No. 783 was fitted with the two chimneys shown, after which a third central chimney was fitted. Besides having only limited success, the results did nothing to enhance the engines' appearance. The most marked effect when working was to dislodge soot from a number of bridges and tunnels as the blast was now hitting them from a different angle. No. 783 reverted to conventional form shortly afterwards.

Collection of A. Molyneaux

THE EMBRYO DESIGN

It was not until 1944, seven years after Bulleid took over on the Southern that the first inklings of a radically new engine began to emerge from the C.M.E.'s department. Bulleid's first thoughts centered on a self-contained locomotive carried on two power bogies.

One could be tempted to ask, why if Bulleid felt so strongly towards the successful development of the steam engine, had it taken until then for the first steps to be taken? Possibly the answer is simply that he needed to establish a reputation for himself, which the appearance of the 'Merchant Navy' and 'Q1' classes certainly achieved. The demands placed upon the railway workshops were now lessening as a successful outcome to war became more clear. In addition Bulleid was a very shrewd individual especially with regard to timing, and no doubt felt that by that date a radically new design would be more likely to find favour compared with when he had first taken office. Another factor in his favour was his personal charisma, certain members of the Southern Board and other senior non-technical officers finding him 'rather clever'.

Accordingly, these first thoughts were translated into drawings by the technical staff from about September 1944 onwards and most rejected purely on the basis of excessive novelty.

Official records refer to the project as first mentioned at the SR board meeting of December 1944, at which Bulleid no doubt wished to place a well formulated idea before

Bulleid's first steam designs for the Southern were the 'Merchant Navy' class, No. 35005 *Canadian Pacific* shown running in early BR days. Apart from some modifications to the front end design to assist in lifting the exhaust clear of the casing, the engine is basically as built.

Collection of A.J. Fry

the directors for their approval. But at this early stage it was not at all clear what Bulleid was trying to achieve, this would not be obvious until some time later.

Therefore the first drawings produced cover a number of machines which were loosely based upon the existing 'Q1' design, and including an 0-6-2T and 0-6-4T. Privately some within the C.M.E.'s department approved of these proposals, as they suggested a powerful machine of conventional design. But closer examination reveals several features that raised questions. One of which was the high axle loading of 19.5 tons which would effectively prohibit the engines from the majority of branch lines, so what was the intended use? This remains an unanswered question. Then there was the question of water consumption, for the high tractive effort of 30,000lbs allied to a 2,000 gallons water capacity would produce a working range of perhaps only 40 miles. (Conclusions on the various early designs were formed on the basis of correspondence and discussion with S.C. Townroe.)

Another disadvantage with the 0-6-4T was its rearward visibility, especially for sighting signals. In addition Bulleid could also foresee other problems, notably the long rigid wheelbase devoid of any guiding wheels, whilst the amount of weight needing to be supported at the rear was a waste of adhesive effort. These factors go some way to suggest why the 0-6-4T has rarely found favour amongst designers.

It therefore appears to indicate that other preoccupations, notably the final details for the new 'Light Pacifics' design, kept the C.M.E. fully occupied, until in late 1944 Bulleid attended one of the regular senior officers meetings at which both the Traffic Manager, R.M.T. Richards and the General Manager, Sir Eustace Missenden were present. Among the items on the agenda was an attempt to decide upon the 1946 locomotive building programme, a particularly difficult task as talk of nationalisation was in the

C16 of the Q1 class shunting at Millbrook during Southern Railway days. Forty engines of the class were built to this Bulleid design from 1942; the lack of running plate and splashers was an obvious departure from the normally accepted practice. Before the first of the engines appeared Bulleid had a wooden model in his office and apparently delighted in the surprise some expressed in seeing the new design. Others though were not so kind and asked, '. . . where does the key go to wind it up . . .?'. The departure from tradition was allegedly dictated by the need to use the minimum of materials. The same care in design was utilized in the Ministry of Supply 2-8-0's, 2-10-0's and 0-6-0T's, but they avoided the sheer ugliness. Appearances aside, the Q1 was a powerful and functional machine, free steaming and generally popular with the crews, although their lack of adequate brake power when working a heavy loose coupled train caused many an anxious moment.

Collection of M. Sumner

offing. During the meeting Richards raised the question of a replacement for the 'M7' tanks, some of which dated back to 1897. His description of the engines is worthy of repeating here: referring to the 'M7's' as ' . . . .completely out of date and inefficient by modern standards, . . . their continued existence prevents any improvement of the services they operate.'

Clearly, what Richard's was after was a large modern tank engine, possibly even the aforementioned 0-6-4T. But instead Bulleid somehow managed to get the Traffic Manager to agree to the building of 25 more 'Q1' tender engines, promising they would be better suited than the existing 'M7's'.

Naturally this was far from satisfactory to Richards and so, possibly prompted by the motive power department who were responsible for maintaining engines in traffic as well as selecting suitable engines for various duties, he wrote to Bulleid on 15 December 1944;

'With regard to your suggestion that the material already available for the construction of Q1 engines should still be used for this type instead of for passenger tanks, an opportunity has been taken of inspecting locomotive No.

The engine type 'Leader' was intended to replace, an M7 tank, seen at Waterloo awaiting what may well be a Clapham Junction working. No. 319 was built in August 1900, one of a batch of five engines constructed to order No. B10. The class originally consisted of 105 engines, the majority built at Nine Elms and rated at a nominal tractive effort of 19,755lbs. The design was simple with few frills, something that certainly could not be said for their intended replacement, 'Leader'. In the event No. 30319, as she became under BR, outlasted 'Leader' by some years and was finally withdrawn in January 1960.

Lens of Sutton

C1 and the conclusion has been arrived at that the lookout facilities provided on this engine are not suitable for regular tender first running. The rear lookout on the driver's side does not give a sufficiently wide range of vision, and the absence of a lookout on the fireman's side is a serious drawback, having regard to the fact that it is necessary for the fireman to assist in looking out for signals when not otherwise necessarily engaged and this is particularly important having regard to the fact that the normal position for signal is on the left-hand side. Unless therefore, the observation conditions, tender first, can be materially improved, I am afraid they will not be suitable to traffic requirements. Another point I would like to raise is as to whether you are satisfied that these engines are suitable for maintaining the necessary speeds running tender first when light in coal and water.'

The last sentence is a reference to a lightly loaded tender 'hunting' from side to side, a valid point, and one which Richard's would be aware of no doubt. Bulleid on the other hand had been involved mainly in workshop practice throughout his professional life. He had no outdoor experience, either as a District Traffic or Motive Power Officer.

With hindsight it is easy to see that Bulleid was playing for time, he had yet to formulate definite plans for the new design and so by obtaining sanction for 25 new 'Q1' engines he had at least got permission to build something for the future.

Meanwhile the test section of the C.M.E.'s department were instructed to conduct some fast test runs using the 'Q1' class. These were made over the former South Eastern main line between Ashford and Maidstone and involved 'Q1' No. C36 attached to a Pacific tender. It was hoped this would improve the rearward visibility of the engines but as the results of these trials have not been found the results cannot be known. A further step was to instruct the drawing office to design a means of duplicating the controls against the tender for rearward running but this did not prove possible by pure mechanical means.

Following a series of private meetings Bulleid and Richards next made a joint approach to Missenden early in 1945 at which the following proposition was made with regard to the 1946 engine requirements:–

> 25 passenger tank engines.
> 10 shunters.
> 25 'West Country' passenger tender engines.

(It subsequently transpired that 14 small 0-6-0T's were purchased for use as shunters from the U.S. Army Transportation Corps for £2,500 each whilst 32 West Country engines were built in the same year.)

However, early in 1945 Britain was still at war and as a result constraints were placed upon available supplies of steel. So even though locomotive building was taken as a necessity each new order was examined by the Ministry of Supply. Even so it was still necessary for the Southern directors to approve of the scheme and to assist them in reaching a decision advice was available from the General Manager.

Missenden then wrote a note to both Bulleid and Richards:

> '. . . . I think we might, pending a decision being reached on the question of the passenger tank engines, indicate at the next M & E Committee that our building programme will be 25 mixed traffic, 25 freight and 10 shunting engines.'

The General Manager was in effect sitting on the fence, no doubt aware of the increasing tension between his C.M.E. and traffic manager, by this then he sought to appease the situation. He was also acutely aware of the performance of the original 'Pacifics' and so perhaps apprehensive about another new and untried design. Accordingly the term 'mixed traffic' was nicely non-commital. (See Appendix B)

In the meantime the drawing office were still busy with various proposed designs, and in March 1945 produced a 'Q1' type of 0-6-0 but with Pacific type cowlings to both the front of the engine and rear of the tender. This was intended to be suitable for either direction running – presumably the difficulties with duplicating controls had been overcome although this is not mentioned.

Shortly afterwards came a variety of large tank engines, including a 2-6-2T, 2-6-4T and finally a 4-6-4T. But the latter design would have suffered from the same disadvantage as the earlier 0-6-4T with regard to wasted weight for adhesion while the high centre of gravity would be likely to preclude fast running. (The Southern were still acutely aware of the consequences of the Sevenoaks' accident in 1927 in which a tank engine at the head of an express was derailed with serious loss of life. From that time on large tank engines were hardly in favour and the Maunsell 'W' class 2-6-4T design of 1931 were prohibited from working passenger trains.)

Bulleid was also quick enough to realise the strength of opposition to these proposals and so now took the design to its logical conclusion by combining the advantages of both tank and tender engines, namely a steam engine on two power bogies. The result was a

In June 1946 there emerged from Brighton the first of the 'Light Pacifics', the class eventually extending to some 110 engines. Externally they were similar to the larger Merchant Navy's, although by the time this view was taken in 1948 certain changes had been made to the design of the cab. Years afterwards, when the Southern Region had a fleet of 140 Bulleid Pacific's, all the earlier Southern built 4-6-0's were also still in service, a surprising fact when in the normal course of events an influx of new engines would be expected to consign an equivalent number to scrap. The reason was the unreliability of the new design. At times splendid to ride on with plenty of steam to spare, master of any job and yet at others totally the reverse. In addition they were very expensive in coal, water, oil and maintainance. One senior official quoting, '. . . oil, oil all over the system'. Depot maintainance staff disliked the engines for their inaccessible moving parts and consequent unreliability in service. This culminated in the decision to rebuild the engines on more conventional lines from 1956 onwards.

Lens of Sutton

C-C type although still with many unanswered engineering problems. Of these the foremost was how would there be room for the steam and exhaust pipes to clear no less than 18 cylinders? Similarly it was unlikely the boiler could produce the steam required and consequently the 3000 gallons of water to be carried would be sufficient for perhaps only 50 miles.

Apart from this first radical new design Bulleid was also faced with opposition from within his own department. His able Chief Draughtsman, C.S. Cocks, who had come with Bulleid from the LNER, far from shared the ideas of his chief. Consequently Cocks attempted to dissuade any further progress towards such a new and untried machine.

Possibly Bulleid could perhaps already sense victory and so approached Richards with a view to finding out his exact requirements for a new engine. The result was a well known memo dated 3.8.45, although probably produced by some hard pressed clerk;

ROUTES AND WEIGHTS OF TRAINS TO BE HAULED

Plymouth to Tavistock or Okehampton	256 tons
Okehampton, Halwill Junction and Bude	256 tons
Barnstaple and Ilfracombe	325 tons

Exeter and Exmouth	384 tons
Bournemouth and Swanage	320 tons
Brookwood, or similar outlying stabling grounds to Waterloo	450 tons

SPEED OF TRAINS 50–60 MILES PER HOUR

DISTANCES TO BE RUN BETWEEN TAKING WATER AND COAL
60 miles for water and 120 miles for coal.

This was hardly an accurate forecast of traffic requirements on the first five lines mentioned. Apart from a few summer Saturdays these routes were the province of light trains on unexacting schedules.

It is therefore the last catagory that is the most interesting. The little 'M7' tanks were having to struggle in and out of Waterloo with empty rakes of perhaps 10, 12 or even 14 coaches and were totally unsuited to the task.

One is left to ponder on Richards' exact thoughts at the time. Irritated no doubt, he may well have thought '. . . all I want is a replacement for those clapped out M7's which slip and slide whenever it is wet and consequently delay everything else. I have been telling him this for months, why can't he just get on with it . . . ?'

It is worth mentioning at this point that apart from the M7's, a host of other engines displaced from more exacting duties were also working many of the duties described above. The 'withered arm', the common title given to the Southern lines west of Exeter, was the home of a motley collection of antiquated designs, most dating back to the 19th century but still perfectly capable of working the poorly patronised services. Yet only a

One of the 14 shunters purchased from the U.S. Transportation Corps for use as dock shunters by the Southern Railway. No. 1974 is depicted outside Eastleigh works in April 1947. Arguably this design could have served as a replacement for the M7's out of Waterloo far better than 'Leader'.

Collection of A. Molyneaux

few years later the appearance of so many 'Light Pacifics' meant these were to be seen on two and three coach trains over the same routes. It was not until the introduction of the BR Standard class '2', '3', and '4' tanks from 1952 onwards that a really efficient machine was available to the traffic department. Exactly the sort of engine everyone hoped Bulleid would produce.

Thus in terms of power requirements Bulleid now had clear criteria for the new design and so began to emerge a steady stream of ideas he considered worthy of inclusion. Other ideas were suggested involving a reduction in the number of classes of steam engine required. It was envisaged that all traffic would be able to be handled by the 'Merchant Navy', 'West Country' and 'Q1' classes together with two types of tank. A little later this was taken one stage further when two versions of 'Leader' were referred to, the design for the prototype No. 36001 as the smaller of the two! But this was pure ideology, for with something in the order of 2000 steam locomotives then running on the Southern the economics of such a suggestion were totally impractical.

However, to return again to 1945, for despite the problems raised by a twin bogie steam engine having multiple cylinders, the possible attractions were enough for Bulleid to set one of his drawing office staff, W.H. 'Joe' Hutchinson on an investigation of the 'sleeve valve' principle which would be ideal on space grounds for a multi-cylinder locomotive.

The sleeve valve also offered other advantages in relation to the supposed thermal efficiency, although against this was an increase in the number of moving parts and known difficulty in lubricating the working surfaces in contact.

Possibly this attraction stemmed from the fact that the earlier Paget design had used similar valves, whilst the sleeve valve was then in regular use on both stationary engines and within the Hawker *Typhoon* aircraft.

Cocks, however, again attempted to bring Bulleid back to more conventional thinking and so the appearance in November 1945 of a further 4-6-4T may well have been associated with him. But again there are variations to the norm, for example a 350 p.s.i. boiler and only two cylinders, although there was no indication as to the type of valves to be used. Shortly after this, in December 1945, Bulleid's influence once again becomes clear with another 4-6-4T, but this time with an offset boiler allowing access to a cab at each end. Oil fuel too was envisaged.

Thus 1946 started with no new design either approved or likely to be so in the immediate future. Left to Cocks the final design may well have been similar to one of the earlier proposals. A conventional tank engine utilising the 'Q1' boiler and capable of a high power output. Bulleid though once again ventured into the unknown, the next design to appear was described by his son H.A.V. Bulleid, as 'The boiler on a well wagon'. Again there were numerous unanswered engineering features.

The concept of this design was now apparent for by February 1946 a second 0-4-4-0 had been suggested, this time with a water tube boiler. Was this latter feature perhaps a throwback to the experimental 'Hush-Hush' engine on the LNER? Certainly Bulleid would have been acquainted with the design.

But these proposals were just that – proposals, without recourse to important details such as axle loadings. The 0-4-4-0 having an unacceptable axle weight of 20 tons compared with the 18 tons of the M7 it was intended to replace.

By now however, Bulleid felt he was winning and so pressed ahead regardless of the reservations of others. At the same time this haste meant he would occasionally 'forget' to liaise with the motive power department regarding the practicalities of his design. Such a lack of consultation, together with, at times, an unpredictable and off-hand manner understandably made him unpopular. He would for example override a subordinates authority in front of junior staff both in the drawing office and on the workshop floor. Apart from the resultant bad feeling, this also caused rifts between men and departments, some of which failed to heal until he left the railway altogether. There was, however, another side to Bulleid which should not be forgotten and it was one by which he is recalled by the numerous artisans at the various running sheds. This shows him to be a genuine, caring man, who through his designs intended to make working conditions as pleasant as possible, while at the same time producing a machine capable of tackling everything that could be reasonably expected of it.

The design was now at a stage where it was a relatively straightforward progression to the adoption of a three axle bogie with a corresponding increase in overall length. Beside better weight distribution this also allowed for a boiler and firebox of suitable size.

April 1946 produced the first of the 0-6-6-0 designs again with the provision for oil fueling.

But as has been shown before, Bulleid was seemingly unable to remain satisfied with anything for long. For this latest drawing contained a hint as to the possible inclusion of condensing apparatus to the 'Holcroft–Anderson' design. Somewhat suprising in view of the abortive tests carried out on the Southern using this system in 1930–5.

This first 0-6-6-0 was in reality a compromise. An engine with conventional piston valves, 4ft. 1in. wheels and a boiler pressure of 280 p.s.i., yet still with a water tube firebox. The inclusion of the third axle on each bogie meant the axle loading was reduced to an admirable 16.15T., although this had to be offset against the length of the monster, 62ft. 6in., similar to most coaches. This was especially so when contrasted against the M7 class maximum of 36ft. 3in., and even more so when seen as an M7 replacement working in and out of such a restricted layout as Waterloo.

Shortly afterwards Bulleid attended another of the regular meetings with the Traffic Manager. This time Richards raised the need for additional locomotives for use on the cross-London freight workings much of which were worked by the 'W' class tanks. Bulleid reportedly listened to the request in silence and then in an outburst so typical of the man proclaimed, '. . . you don't really want them, because they are confined to one class of duty. What you need is a substantially more powerful mixed traffic tank locomotive with full route availability.'

In practice this would not have been feasible, for if Bulleid had bothered to investigate further he would have found that at times five hours or more could be spent at Brent or Willesden waiting for the LMS yard staff to make up a train for the return journey. It was just not possible to diagram an engine for another duty elsewhere when such unpredictable timings were involved. As the fault was not of the Southerns' making there was little scope for possible improvement.

So why did Bulleid continue with what was already such a complicated design? The answer must lie in his own forceful character, his stubborn insistence that the continuation of development was not only desirable but essentially necessary for the future motive power requirements of the Southern Railway. How the directors ever came to sanction this further development of steam, especially in view of their publicly avowed policy towards electrification, must remain the subject of conjecture.

As with the earlier 'Merchant Navy's', Bulleid thus set himself the criteria and ideals his new locomotive should reach. 'An all round performer capable of handling passenger and goods trains normally taken by the West Country and Q1 class engines and able to reach speeds of 90 mph.' He went on to state that there should also be a reduction in the maintainance required. The last statement was one with which no doubt every locomotive designer would wish to concur. Indeed these ideals had already been displayed in certain aspects of his previous ventures but, as already recalled, in practice the reverse was often the case.

With assured confidence Bulleid next wrote to the General Manager;

> Sir Eustace Missenden, 11.7.1946
>
> In order to meet these requirements (referring to the original dictate of the Traffic Manager) within the limits imposed by the Chief Civil Engineer as regards permanent way and bridges. I propose a locomotive in accordance with the enclosed diagram. The engine will have a maximum speed of 90 mph and will be able to work goods trains which are normally taken by the Q1 and passenger trains equal to the 'West Country' engines, and will carry at least sufficient water and coal to run 80 miles between taking water and 150 miles without taking coal.
> The engine weights are so distributed as to enable it to run over the whole of the Company's lines with the following exceptions;
>
> > Wenford Bridge line
> > Hayling Island Branch
> > Bere Alston and Callington
> > Rye Harbour Branch
> > Newhaven Swing Bridge
> > Dover, Prince of Wales Pier
> > Axminster and Lyme Regis Branch
> > Isle of Wight lines
> > – none of which is important
>
> It is estimated that, if a batch of 25 engines of this class were built, cost per engine would be £17,000. If one prototype was built, the cost would obviously be greater, dependant upon the development work found necessary during construction and might reach £25,000.'

It was now up to the directors to hopefully sanction approval. Bulleid used the time to continue on a number of variations to the drawings. Again the 0-6-6-0 concept was used but this time the wheelbase was lengthened so that a 70ft. turntable would have been required – at that time there were few of these on the Southern!

In addition a dry back boiler with thermic syphons was proposed whilst sleeve valves were shown to be incorporated.

The dry back boiler itself may be more correctly described as a conventional boiler attached to a firebox in which only the crown (or top) is covered by water. Both sides and back being of plain metal and again similar to the Paget engine. The thermic syphons were to assist in water circulation to and from the crown, two of which had already been incorporated in the Pacific firebox but allied to conventional principles. In the new design there would be no less than four syphons and so provide the maximum available surface space for heat transfer in what was the hottest part of the engine. In this way the resultant loss of heating surface due to the 'dry-sides' could be offset. It was a commendable effort and a major stage towards Bulleid's avowed aim of reduced maintainance. The inclusion of the dry sides compared with a conventional stayed firebox counterbalanced by no loss of firebox efficiency.

Bulleid took the first steps towards a patent for his new design on 2.9.46, but it was not until 21.1.49 that Patent No. 616.445 was issued covering 'Improvements relating to locomotive and like steam boilers.'

The inclusion of sleeve valves was a direct result of Hutchinson's drawings. A modification to the standard sleeve valve principle was also envisaged in that a degree of axial rotation was imparted during the stroke and intended to reduce the likelihood of seizure. (This modification was at the suggestion of Sir Harry Ricardo whose engine-ering company at Shoreham had conducted much research into the sleeve valve principle.)

Aesthetically the ends of the engine now took on a decidedly rounded appearance, not unlike the Pacifics which in turn were similar to contemporary French styling. In part this was due to the increased front overhang dictated by the use of sleeve valves which were in themselves relatively long and thin. The overall length was shown as no less than 66ft.

With new ideas flowing on an almost daily basis one can almost imagine Bulleid impatiently awaiting final authorisation to proceed. This came one step closer on 4 September when a meeting of 'The Rolling Stock (Repair and Renewals) Progress Committee' was held at Waterloo. The latest drawings were made available to the meeting along with a descriptive memo from the C.M.E. himself.

LEADING CLASS. SHUNTING ENGINE. C-C TYPE

The principle features of the new engine are as follows;

This design of engine makes full and complete use of the total weight for adhesive purposes and braking. The type of bogie is similar to that introduced on the electric locomotive, the riding of which has been found to be satisfactory. The springs and gear will be above the axleboxes and under continuous lubrication. The whole of the moving parts will be enclosed and fitted with automatic lubrication, so that it will not be necessary for the driver to lubricate any part of the machine. Each engine will have three 'simple' cylinders driving the intermediate axle. The load is transmitted to the leading and trailing axles by chain drive in an oiltight casing. Roller bearing boxes will be fitted to all axles and will receive force feed lubrication. The axleboxes will be contained in an oilbath. Each axlebox guide is fitted with a 'Silentbloc' bearing. The leading engine will exhaust to atmosphere, by way of the blast pipe in the smokebox, so as to provide the necessary draught in the boiler, but exhaust from the trailing engine will be used to heat the water in the tank, the hot water being pumped to the boiler by suitable hot water pumps. The boiler is a new design which will obviate the maintainance inherent in the normal type of locomotive boiler. The engine will also be fitted with feed water treatment incorporated in the tender. The controls of the engine will be such that both men will be able to carry out their duties seated and will be duplicated where necessary, so that they can drive in either direction. The weight of water and fuel indicated should be ample for the normal requirements of the Southern Railway, espe-cially as by condensing steam from one engine, the water consumption should be appreciably reduced. The engine is fitted with 5ft. 1in. wheels and this in conjunction with the short stroke, will allow the engine to run at speeds up to 90 mph, without exceeding the normal piston speed. The engine will not be air-smoothed in any sense of the word, but the front end will be based on that sucessfully introduced on the 'West Country' class engines, in order to ensure that the steam, when the engine is working lightly, is carried clear of the cab.

This was the first time the project had been officially referred to as the 'Leading Class', possibly the idea of the Public Relations Department, but from it of course came the connotation 'Leader'. Mention is also made of 'simple' cylinders and this ought perhaps to be explained in the light of the previous references to sleeve valves. Simple cylinders refer to the use of steam for expansion once only before exhausting to the blast pipe or pre-heating the feed. It matters not as to the design of valves used to control the entry and exit of the steam into the cylinders and indeed over the years a number of different types had been used in the steam locomotive.

Another anomaly relates to the statement that both the crew would be able to perform their duties seated. As far as this refers to the driver it is easy to explain, but hand-firing a locomotive from a seated position is impossible for any length of time. It is all the more difficult to explain as by this time all references to oil firing are missing from the drawings whilst there is similarly no reference to mechanical stoking.

Finally the mention of feed pumps and pre-heating, which was a far from new idea. In this way overall efficiency was raised but at the expense of added mechanical complications and in a country where water is a plentiful commodity it is unlikely any worthwhile savings could be accrued. Possibly though Bulleid hoped to carry less water, and use what was carried in a more efficient way so saving on weight. (2500 gallons of water weighs approx 11.5 tons.) But whatever the reason the proposal was dropped. It is the opinion of the author that this was possibly partly due to a desire to incorporate T.I.A. water treatment which would be upset by the presence of particles of lubricating oil in the condensed water.

To the frustration of the C.M.E. no immediate decision was given to proceed, although it was minuted that '. . . an early decision was desirable.' This was in no small part due to a representative of the Superintendent of Operations Department arguing with some passion against the prospect of some twenty five new machines which comprised so many ' . . . unorthodox and untried ideas', and suggesting instead that trials be carried out with only one prototype. Conservatism or knowledgeable caution?

Bulleid, however, was not to be so easily put off and continued in his attempt to push through his ideas. Most of the committee were also non-technical and he used this to advantage. An understandable compromise was then reached, five engines were to be built. Hardly satisfactory to the Traffic Manager who still awaited his replacement for the M7's.

The following day confirmation of the decision arrived.

From the General Manager;
    To the Chief Mechanical Engineer.

PROPOSED TANK ENGINE

With reference to Minute 79 of the meeting of the Progress Committee held yesterday, the Traffic Manager informs me that he has had a further discussion with you upon this matter and he now recommends we proceed with the building of five engines to diagram W7326. I shall be glad if you will proceed accordingly.'

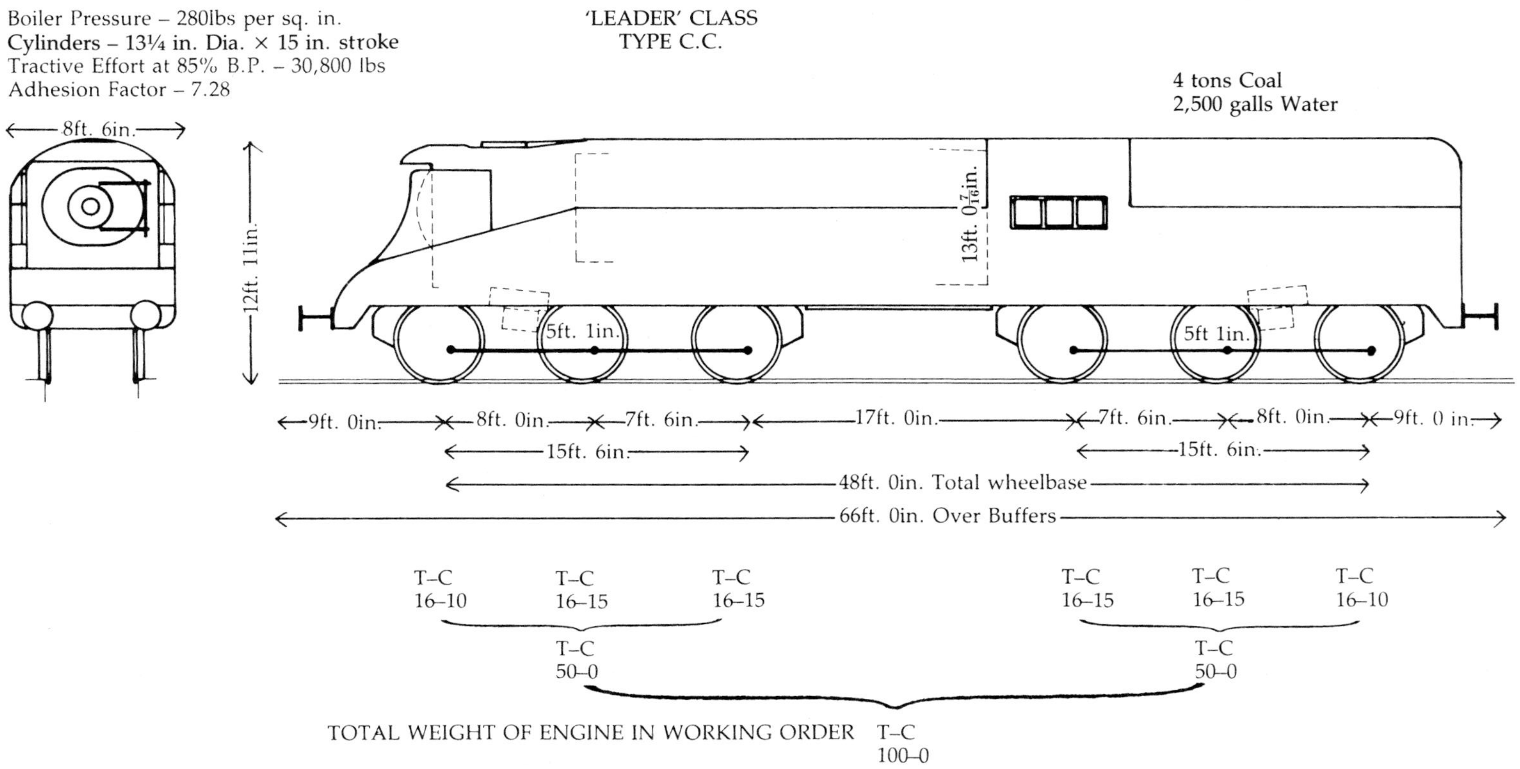

'LEADER' CLASS
TYPE C.C.

Boiler Pressure – 280lbs per sq. in.
Cylinders – 13¼ in. Dia. × 15 in. stroke
Tractive Effort at 85% B.P. – 30,800 lbs
Adhesion Factor – 7.28

4 tons Coal
2,500 galls Water

8ft. 6in.

12ft. 11in.

13ft. 0 7/16 in.

5ft. 1in.

5ft. 1in.

9ft. 0in.

8ft. 0in.

7ft. 6in.

15ft. 6in.

17ft. 0in.

7ft. 6in.

8ft. 0in.

9ft. 0 in.

15ft. 6in.

48ft. 0in. Total wheelbase

66ft. 0in. Over Buffers

T–C
16–10

T–C
16–15

T–C
50–0

T–C
16–15

T–C
16–15

T–C
16–15

T–C
50–0

T–C
16–10

TOTAL WEIGHT OF ENGINE IN WORKING ORDER   T–C
100–0

Presumably the further discussion referred to between Bulleid and Richards centred around the latters' apprehension of likely teething troubles to come.

Matters now progressed rapidly, with an official order, No. 3382 issued to the Brighton Drawing Office on 11.9.46, that simply stated 'Build five tank engines to Diagram W7326.'

Thus there began to emerge the first of hundreds of separate drawings necessary for the new design. Several have survived and are dated either 1946 or 1947 but are unlikely to be of much interest at the present time as they just cover the basic engineering details of the new design.

In the meantime the administrative process ground on with the Traffic Manager submitting his official requirements for the new design to the R.S. (Repair & Renewals) P.C. at Waterloo at the beginning of October.

'In reply to your letter of the 5th. September and referring to minute No 79 of the Progress Committee Meeting held on the 4th September. The case justifying the construction of 25 new passenger tank engines is given below. At the present time and, indeed, for the past 45 years the most powerful passenger tank engines on the Western Section have been those of the M7 class, 104 of which are still in existence. These engines were built between the years 1897–1911 and although the last 49 embody slight improvements, the whole class was based on a design prepared in 1897 and now, therefore, nearly 50 years old. They were originally built for L & SWR suburban traffic and were, in due course, rendered redundant by electrification. They are now being used as general utility locomotives, 25% working empty trains between Clapham Junction, or other stock berthing points and Waterloo, and the balance on local and branch line services on the Western Section. They are completely out of date and inefficient by modern standards, and their continued existence prevents any improvement on the services they operate. In the report to yourself dated 1.12.1944, upon our locomotive position in 1950, prepared by the Deputy General Manager and other Chief Officers, the whole of these 104 engines were condemned, and this recommendation was confirmed in the corresponding report upon the 1955 locomotive position submitted on 3.9.1946. The report dealing with the Engine Building Programme during the years 1947–1955 recommends the building of 60 new tank engines, diesel or steam, in addition to the 25 tanks already proposed, and I now recommend that the latter be constructed. It is understood that the five engines to be built will be a guide as to the building of the subsequent 20.'

(Unfortunately the reports referred to above concerning the locomotive position in 1950 and 1955 have not been traced.)

So why had such a shortage of suitable steam power been allowed to occur? It is not necessary to look far to find the answer – a preoccupation with electrification at the expense of steam.

Meanwhile at a board meeting on 3.10.46 an interesting comment arises;

'Mr. Bulleid also said that only one of the new Passenger Tanks would be completed in June 1947, and that the remaining four would follow as soon as possible thereafter.

The Traffic Manager intimated that from an operating point of view it would be better if the five engines were constructed for coal burning in order to ensure greater mobility, particularly in regard to Depot allocation, and the Chairman requested the Chief Mechanical Engineer to proceed accordingly.'

The opportunity for 'Leader' to be oil fired had been lost, it was the first of many pitfalls that eventually led to the failure of the engine. Certainly matters could perhaps have been rectified had a mechanical stoker been fitted, but no plans to suggest this have been found. It is also worth pointing out that this was at a time when the Government of the day had entered into a commitment for the use of oil fuel on railway locomotives. But to digress further on that particular topic is to become involved in the political arena of the day and it is now time to return again to October 1946 and the further progression of the design.

To the staff of the C.M.E.'s department this was an exciting time, their railway was involved in research into the ultimate steam engine, potentially the most exciting development for decades. But such euphoria was not necessarily universal, for a number of senior staff still expressed a degree of scepticism, fuelled by the fact that the existing Pacific engines spent a considerable amount of time in the works undergoing one modification after another.

Bulleid though was far from restrained and apparently heedless to both the criticism of his Pacific's and calls for caution over 'Leader'. Consequently he pushed ahead and now included as an essential criteria the advantages of a driving cab at each end, so alleviating the need for a turntable at terminal stations.

Accordingly a design was prepared which showed a driving cab at each end but in addition having a corridor connection as well. One is tempted to ask the obvious question, what would this have been for? Surely not as the LNER practice of crew changing en route, as on the Southern even the longest runs were too short a distance to warrant this? Could it possibly have been the first suggestion towards multiple working?

Another feature not shown clearly was the central firing compartment and if it was to have windows on both sides. Nor how the balance was to be restored from placing the boiler offset from the centre line. This last modification would allow access between all three cabs via a narrow corridor. Indeed only a few months later when a senior Brighton Official was asked, 'How are you going to balance the offset boiler?' The reply received was, '. . . that is a good question, we are still trying to discover the answer!' Evidently it was never forthcoming.

Meanwhile at the Brighton drawing office there was feverish activity, although outside the confines of the works little was known. Understandably rumours were rife, these sometimes provoking the comment that the footplate crews would object to working in enforced solitude. Presumably none of these critics had recourse to consider the existing push–pull arrangements or single manning of electric units.

Then in December 1946 the first orders for material were placed with various outside suppliers. It was also realised that the project was now not only a challange to technical advancement but also a race against time with nationalisation just one year away.

Accordingly, with the drawing office working flat out, the final designs for the sleeve valves were ready in the spring of 1947, while at the same time the advantages of an all welded construction were being investigated. But as already stated, other than in the Paget engine, sleeve valves had had little railway use and so it was wisely decided to convert an existing engine as a 'guinea pig' for the new venture. Eventually an 'H1' – Atlantic was chosen. (See next chapter.)

Bulleid made what was probably the first reference to the 'Leader' project outside the works in June 1947 when he lectured at the Centenary of the Institution of Mechanical Engineers. Referring to the potential advantages of the new design he stated;

> 'A new type of heavy, mixed traffic tank engine is under construction and these engines embody further developments of the innovations introduced in the tender engines, all with the object of developing a steam engine as easy to maintain and operate as possible. As the locomotive is carried on two six-wheeled bogies, the whole weight is available for adhesion and braking and the engine can run over 97 percent of the company's system.'

Bulleid was however, slightly ahead of himself here, simply because construction did not actually start at Brighton until July 1947. The former LBSCR works was used as it was the only one of the three SR workshops with spare capacity for such a project. There were other advantages in using Brighton, for here was the C.M.E.'s head office whilst the works drawing office was responsible for most of the detail drawings.

A more public mention was made concerning the project on 18.10.47 as part of an address Bullied gave to the Institute of Mechanical Engineers, to which body he had recently been elected president. Eight days later an abstract of the paper was published in the journal *Modern Transport* under the title 'New Conception of Steam Locomotive Design – Lessons for the Immediate Future'. An extract from this is shown in Appendix C and clearly shows the character of the designer together with his intentions.

Understandably there was a great deal of interest shown in Bulleid's paper and such enthusiasm was relished within the C.M.E.'s department. This in turn encouraged the flow of ideas, including an interchangable power bogie, another of the inherent advantages of the diesel/electric lobby, although on financial grounds alone a fleet far greater than five engines would have been needed to justify holding spares.

But practical progress was slow with the first set of main frames not completed until May 1948, five months into nationalisation. Indeed throughout the project it would be fair to say certain work was completed on an *ad hoc* basis and apparently without the benefit of drawings, these were either not available or almost impossible to comprehend after numerous amendments.

In the meantime thirty-one more engines to the same design had been authorised in November 1947. But this was purely a pre-nationalisation gesture by the Southern Railway for the order was never confirmed by the Railway Executive.

It was also a close run thing that the original order for just five engines was allowed to proceed, especially as work was nowhere near completion. Indeed questions were already being asked both at Waterloo and 222 Marylebone Road – Headquarters of the Railway Executive, concerning the cost of the project. This was quoted in July 1948 as £87,500 for five engines, subsequently adjusted by the Chief Accountant just two months later to £100,000. These figures were approximately double the cost of constructing a comparatively powered steam locomotive to an existing design. With money short it was understandable that the project became known as 'Bleeder' when reference was made to the escalating costs. One official when asked if he was worried over the finance replied, '. . . worried is not the word.'

Through all the turmoil created by nationalisation Bulleid had been allowed to remain in charge of the project. His ally the former SR General Manager, Sir Eustace Missenden had been elevated to Chairman of the Railway Executive, with the new boss at Waterloo, Sir John Elliot equally sympathetic. But overall charge of mechanical engineering on BR came now under the control of Robin Riddles at Marylebone, and while there was never any question of personal animosity between Bulleid and his senior colleagues, Riddles knew enough of Bulleid to keep a wary eye on his activities.

Had work continued under a private Southern Railway the engine numbering would have been to Bulleid's unusual style, CC101-5, with names likely to have included:

> Missenden, Sir Eustace
> Churchill, Sir Winston
> Montgomery, Field Marshal
> Walker, Sir Hubert

In the event BR allocated Nos. 36001–5 with no vestige of names. As far as is known nameplates were never cast.

Pressure was also being brought to bear to have the engines completed, and so the decision was taken to concentrate resources on the first of the class temporarily at the expense of the remainder. Ironically this meant work pressed ahead on No. 36001 before any necessary lessons learnt from the trials of the converted 'H1' could be incorporated.

Consequently No. 36001 steamed away from Brighton for the first time in late June 1949, two years late and even then still incomplete, as Brighton had complained of difficulties in fitting the multiple valve rings. Bulleid impatiently decided Eastleigh could complete the work.

Much else was different from diagram W7326 of 1946 and on which the approval to go ahead had been based. The offset boiler, position of driving cabs and outer casing are just three examples. The concept of the corridor connections had also disappeared whilst the suggested cowlings at the ends had not materialised. Three windows at each end provided for an uninterupted view of the way ahead.

But what was the way ahead, and where would it lead? Towards a resurgence for steam or the seemingly remorseless march onward of the diesels? Now was the time to watch and ponder on the days ahead.

THE PRELUDE

The experimental engines and *Hartland Point*

With work progressing on No. 36001 at Brighton the opportunity was taken to assess the suitability of some of the features it was hoped to incorporate within the new design.

The first of these involved the fitting of a 'U1' class 2-6-0 No. 1896 with a 6in. square duct in the base of the smokebox through which char and ash could drop to the track. This it was hoped would reduce the problem of the engine smokebox becoming choked with cinders after hard working for some distance and its consequently detrimental effect on steaming.

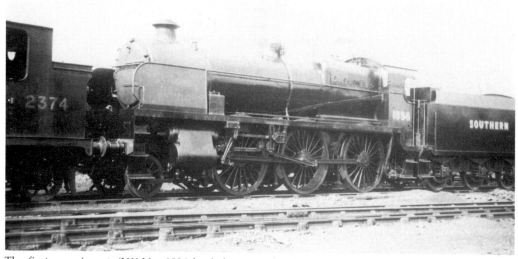

The first experiment, 'U1' No. 1896 fresh from overhaul at Ashford Works in the summer of 1946 and probably at the time the open ash duct was fitted. How such a fitment was physically routed around the centre cylinder of this three cylinder engine is not clear. Almost certainly the ash chute would have been under some form of remote control from the driver, for otherwise with the chute permanently open steaming would have been seriously impaired.

R.C. Riley

Of course if the oil firing of 'Leader' had ever been a serious consideration, such fitments would have been rendered unnecessary. But on the 'Leader' design as it stood the experiment was of considerable importance, for the disposal of hot ash from an enclosed smokebox was rightly recognised as not only an unpleasant but also a potentially dangerous task and certainly one to be avoided if at all possible. There must have been considerable satisfaction then that No. 1896 performed reasonably well, although she was fresh from overhaul.

While this particular experiment may have been new, the same could not be said of the desire to develop a self-cleaning type of smokebox. Indeed many years earlier, J.G. Robinson, as C.M.E. of the Great Central used a series of steam jets within the smokebox which were under the remote control of the driver. Their function was to stir up the ash and direct it upwards into the blast from which it dispersed out of the chimney. This took place at intervals along the journey and consequently when travelling in GCR trains it was common to hear 'hail-stones' on the carriage roof coinciding with the ejection of ashes. An unfortunate side effect was that the legal department of the railway were kept busy with claims where hot cinders were alledgedly responsible for setting fire to property alongside the railway! As the GCR had been absorbed into his former employers, the LNER in 1923, Bulleid would no doubt have been aware of this early work.

Already one question arises, why did Bulleid start these experiments when some years earlier the LNER had fitted the same type of open duct in the smokebox and which

A self-cleaning smokebox on a former GWR 'King' class engine photographed at Swindon during BR days. The mesh screens were removable so as to afford access to the tubes and blastpipe. Similar screens were fitted by BR to a number of engines from 1951 onwards.

'R.A.' Collection

had already been proven to be a failure. The problem being that despite the duct supposedly being able to be closed by remote action from the cab, ash and char would prevent a secure fit and consequently air continued to be drawn into the usual vacuum of the smokebox and thereby impaired steaming.

Ironically a few years later BR were to fit fine mesh screens within the smokebox of a number of engines and with considerable success. These performed the task of preventing the char from falling to the floor, being caught instead in the blast before being successfully ejected from the chimney.

HARTLAND POINT

As previously referred to briefly, it was decided to test the proposed sleeve valve principle in service and the search began for a suitable guinea pig engine. This was after a preliminary quarter scale model of the adapted Bulleid valve gear associated with sleeve valves was made and which gave good valve event timing.

The C.M.E.'s department eventually selected a Marsh Atlantic of the 'H1' class for the trials. No. 2039 *Hartland Point* was taken into Brighton works in July 1947. The choice of this engine is particularly interesting, for it is alleged that the first preference had been that of a 'King Arthur' class locomotive. But the use of one of these machines allied to the new cylinders dictated by the inclusion of sleeve valves, and coupled to the same size pistons as before, would have fouled the loading gauge. There would have been no reason why smaller pistons could not have been used, although it has also been suggested that the Motive Power Department were reluctant at the thought of giving up what was a reliable straight-forward engine.

No. 454 *Queen Guinevere* of the King Arthur class portrayed outside Exmouth Junction shed. Despite a member of this class being ruled out for conversion to sleeve valves, Bulleid did successfully modify many of the type with a multiple jet blast pipe and wide diameter chimney. No. 454 is shown before any such modification and also displays to advantage the high standard of external cleanliness once commonplace on the railways.

Lens of Sutton

There were five engines in the H1 class, built as Nos. 37–41 by Messrs Kitson between December 1905 and February 1906; their ancestry from the design of the earlier Great Northern Atlantics is clearly discernable. No. 39 is shown in almost original condition complete with bogie brakes which were later removed. When selected for conversion by Bulleid there were strong views over the choice of this particular machine. One being that sister engine No. 2037 should have been selected as she was always a shy steamer. Nos. 2038 and 2039 were seen as the best of the class and by converting one it was regarded as a waste of a good engine.

Collection of Les Warnett

The Atlantic however was on the short list for scrapping. Certainly with time at a premium the choice of 2039 was no doubt based on the simplicity of the original design, although it is also interesting to reflect that one of Bulleid's existing types was not selected.

Accordingly with No. 2039 due for withdrawal the decision was made to sacrifice piston diameter for compatability within the loading gauge. As a result the actual piston size was reduced from 19in. to 14in., although the stroke remained constant at 26 in. with the crankpins unaltered. This meant that with the 6ft. 7in. wheels fitted the nominal tractive effort was reduced from 20,070lbs to 11,892lbs – assessed at 85% b.p.

MECHANICAL WORK

Work on the conversion involved an almost complete rebuild of the front end. As apart from the new cylinders a multiple jet blast pipe was fitted together with the well known Bulleid large diameter chimney. The Westinghouse air pump was also resited to the right hand side of the smokebox.

For both ease and quickness of manufacture the outer casing of the new cylinders was in the form of a fabricated steel shell. Around the outside was welded a central 'live' steam annulus, flanked by an exhaust steam annulus at either end. A cast 'Mechanite' (fine grain cast iron) liner was pressed into the cylinder to provide a working bearing surface for the sleeve valve which was itself basically a partial tube of Mechanite. The actual sleeve was machined to a sliding fit and sealed with 30 separate rings.

No. 2039 during the course of conversion in Brighton Works. This is the right hand cylinder, although yet to be attached are the connections from the sleeve lugs to the oscillating gear. Note the running plate has been removed from behind the cylinder as far as the buffer beam. A number of components including the new bogie are yet to be added.

National Railway Museum

The machined inside diameter of the sleeve formed a cylinder in which a normal type of piston worked. At either end separate steam and exhaust ports were machined around the periphery of both sleeve and liner and so allowed steam to travel between the respective annulus and cylinder proper.

Each sleeve was provided with two integrally cast extension lugs which protruded through the front cylinder cover. These were bridged by a machined steel cross-bar bolted between each lug. Steam was admitted to each cylinder via a central joint on the top face of the cylinder and to which a short length of round steel tube, set inward, provided the connection to prefabricated protrusions welded to the outside walls of the circular smokebox. Although not aesthetically pleasing it was probably the most practical method, after all *Hartland Point* was essentially a mobile test bed. Two exhaust connections were made by equally practical if ugly means.

The increase in overall length of the new cylinders meant the existing 3ft. 6in. diameter bogie wheels were fouled. This was overcome by substituting the bogie with one from a 'D3' 0-4-4 tank with 3ft. wheels.

The valve events were controlled as before by an internal Stephenson's link motion. The valve rods were connected to plungers and guide bushes pressed into a fabricated steel stretcher bolted between the frames. This stretcher was itself in the space originally occupied by the inside steam chests.

To transmit the drive to the outside of the frames, a rocking lever was mounted either side, each pivoted in a substantial bushed steel housing bolted to the outside face of the frame. The outer links drove rearwards and were attached to each of the sleeve cross-bars where connection was made by universal ball-type joints. This was to absorb the independant oscillating drive. The latter was itself obtained from a rotating camshaft sprocket driven by a 'Morse' inverted tooth chain from the leading coupled axle.

Right hand cylinder and sleeve showing the connections to the oscillating gear from the extended sleeve 'ears'. In the top right corner one of the two mechanical lubricators is visible, although the position of both of these beneath the smokebox door was far from ideal. This location of course was subject to a liberal covering of ash and cinders every time the smokebox was cleaned. The mass of exposed oil pipes is only too apparent, the whole appearance typifying the engine as an experimental venture.

Derek Clayton

The shaft was mounted in bearings located on both main frames, through which they protruded to terminate with an eccentric flange on either end. The flange worked in a horizontal slot provided in a bearing block bolted to the outside radius of the inner sleeve lub. Thus as the sleeve was made to reciprocate and so provide the valve events, an oscillating motion was imparted to facilitate lubrication and even out wear. The sleeve performed a 'figure of eight' movement which was reputedly fascinating to watch.

THE WHY AND THE WHEREFORE

Bulleid's object in employing a sleeve valve cylinder design was to obtain a marked increase in thermal efficiency. Theoretically this would certainly be higher than that procured from a conventional slide or piston valve engine as with sleeve valves the cylinders would suffer less condensation. This was because the steam and exhaust annulia would keep the cylinder temperature both higher and more constant during each stroke. A large steam chest (or steam charge) volume of 3¼ times the cylinder volume at maximum cut-off would also result from the large steam admission annuli. Increased steam flow could then be expected, similar facilities allowed for a free flowing exhaust.

However loss of mechanical efficiency had to be offset against the improved thermal advantages. This was due to the high frictional losses attributed to maintaining a steam tight seal across the exhaust ports and the front radial outlet slots for the extension drive lugs.

27

In an attempt to reduce this to a minimum a large number of oil feed connections were made along the upper faces of the cylinders. Accordingly generous pressure lubrication was available to the large bearing surfaces and multitude of sealing rings on the sleeves. Two 'Wakefield' mechanical lubricators, chain driven, were mounted between the frames ahead of the smokebox and pumped oil via a network of copper pipes and connectors.

With the need for accessibility whilst undergoing trials, together with the difficulty of fitting the running plates around the top entry steam and exhaust connections, the running plates were terminated at the rear end of the cylinders. Together with the mass of exposed pipes and oil feeds this feature did much to alter the previously graceful outline of the original Marsh design.

THE TESTS WITH No. 2039

Unlike the later runs with 'Leader', the trials of No. 2039 are referred to only briefly in official records and consequently it is not certain that a full record of all runs and tests was compiled.

What is believed to have been the first steaming of the modified engine took place on 5.11.47, although this was probably only a preliminary shop test. At this stage no rings had been fitted to the sleeves so there was considerable steam leakage from the front end. Following this came a series of works tests, one on 3.12.47 witnessed by Bulleid's brother-in-law, H.G. Ivatt, where the engine was reported as running well but still shrouded in escaping steam from the front end.

No. 2039 then re-entered the works for the fitting of the necessary piston rings, following which on 15.12.47 she was noted in steam, first outside the works and then later the same day at the nearby Brighton running shed. The same afternoon a trip was made to Lewes in company with 'E5' tank No. 2404, the operating authorities obviously taking no chances of failure with a new and untried design. A short visit was then necessary to the works to replace a number of broken rings, while before the end of December some further tests were again made to Lewes.

The first day of the new year in 1948, and coincidently the first day of nationalised ownership of the railways, found No. 2039 working between Brighton and Eastbourne on empty stock formed with ex-SECR 3-car set No. 597. Although not carrying passengers, the train made a brief halt at each of the stations en route, the purpose of which was to gauge the acceleration characteristics of the engine in its modified form. Evidently all was well for there followed daily tests from Brighton to Groombridge via Lewes, a distance of some 30 miles. It was said on these duties the engine was very free running and reached a reputed 70–80 mph with ease. .

In addition there were a number of light engine runs, mainly to Three Bridges, one at least with a 'K' class mogul being propelled in both directions.

It would certainly seem that results from these early trials were promising, for in February 1948, No. 2039 appeared at Eastleigh on an empty stock train from the carriage works at Lancing. Several further runs between Eastleigh and Lancing followed, in this way at least No. 2039 performed a useful role to the traffic department. By the end of the month though the engine was again back at Brighton and receiving attention in the works.

Between March and June 1948 there were a series of runs from Brighton to either Lewes or Cowden. Also in June a 3-coach set was worked between Brighton and Tunbridge Wells West and return, after which the destination was changed to Hastings, but still with the same trailing load. The series of tests concluded with a twice daily run at the head of a 4–5 coach set again to Tunbridge Wells which lasted sometime into July.

No. 2039 leaving Brighton for Groombridge on a test train. Trials were usually commenced from the passenger station so as to simulate as near as possible realistic working. In this way it was also possible to afford a direct comparison in running times.

P. Ransom Wallis/National Railway Museum

Details for the next couple of months are obscure but in September 1948, No. 2039 was seen at the head of a train of bogie utility vans after which the engine once more re-entered the works.

She was not to emerge again until early December 1948, and now on a series of light engine trials on the coast line as far as Hastings. Two trips were made each way and mainly at weekends. Perhaps because of previous successes, 19.12.48 saw the engine at the head of an Officers special from Ashford to Brighton. Unfortunately on leaving St. Leonards disaster struck with a sudden fracture of the right hand valve rod. The motion had to be taken down in the nearby shed yard followed by an ignominious tow back to Brighton.

No. 2039's next known outing was on 14.3.49, the Motive Power Department seemingly having enough faith to entrust the engine to a public passenger train. However, in view of the lack of use in the previous three months, it was more likely to be pressure exerted from other quarters that prompted such movement. Whatever the reasons No. 2039 was set to take the three coaches of the Hastings–Birkenhead through service between Brighton and Redhill, the task being accomplished without difficulty. The return working was also successfully achieved later the same day.

Two days later the engine was rostered for a further trip to Redhill, but this time on three empty coaches from Brighton. All was well until Earlswood was reached, just short of her destination, where No. 2039 was to totally disgrace herself. Apparently the free running capabilities and light load had resulted in an earlier than anticipated arrival

No. 2039 at Uckfield, again on a test working. Unlike 'Leader' it is not believed the reciprocating mechanism of the sleeves was ever removed. The lack of a headcode of any sort is obvious.
P. Ransom Wallis/National Railway Museum

so a signal check was encountered. The problem came when the signal cleared, the engine refusing to start, moving neither forward or back. It later transpired that the steam ports around the sleeve were inaccurately placed, although it is not clear if this was due to a fault in design, manufacture or setting.

While the crew struggled valiantly to persuade No. 2039 to move a pilot engine was urgently sought, and after 25 minutes the complete failure was hauled the short distance to Redhill. The return to Brighton later in the day was in company with 'E' class 4-4-0 No. 31587.

As previously recounted there is little background information available showing known modifications and repairs, so one can only speculate on any repairs that must have been carried out. But work there certainly was, for on 1.4.49, No. 2039 again ventured out at the head of a 3-coach special to Ashford. It was soon apparent that there were still difficulties, for following a signal stop at Ore it took 7½ minutes to restart, somewhat unfortunate as both Bulleid and a member of his senior staff were present on the footplate. Perhaps a more suitable day should have chosen for the test!

Whatever the impression gained it was not enough to prevent further runs, as a short time later No. 2039 was again at the head of a works train between Lancing and Eastleigh.

The original intention had been to return No. 2039 to her original form as soon as No. 36001 was completed, but this was never done, no doubt because of her anticipated short future life. Accordingly following a period of open store at Brighton she entered the works on 14.6.49. The focus of attention now transferred away from No. 2039 towards 'Leader' herself who was rapidly nearing completion.

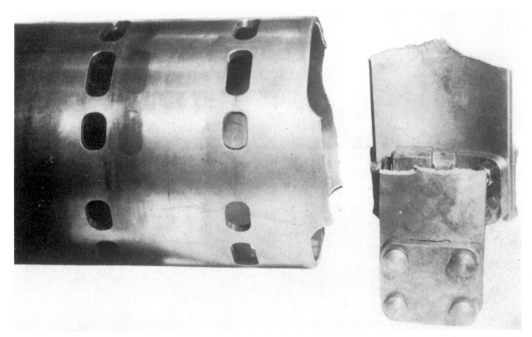

A broken sleeve extracted from No. 2039 possibly following the failure at St. Leonards on 19.12.48. The number of runs made light engine indicate the varying degrees of success associated with the trials. The discolouration along part of the length of the sleeve is an indication of seizure, possibly caused by lack of adequate lubrication, which may well have contributed to this particular failure.

National Railway Museum

No. 2039 languished for most of the summer within the works, perhaps awaiting a decision as to her future. Eventually the choice was made and amidst a degree of surprise she was given a 'heavy intermediate' overhaul which even included fitting a replacement boiler sent especially from Eastleigh. The engine emerged from Brighton as BR No. 32039 *Hartland Point* on 3.9.49 still with the sleeve valves and she was allocated to Brighton shed shortly afterwards.

There now followed a period of some 16 months during which any movements of the engine are not clear. Possibly much of this time was spent in store although the economic sense of this following an expensive overhaul are open to question.

Drawing purely on what would seem to be likely and is therefore conjecture, it must be said that No. 32039 was not in a reliable enough condition to work in normal traffic. The engine was considerably less powerful than others of her type and the retention of the sleeve valves meant her reputation was still open to question. Accordingly with all eyes focussed on No. 36001, *Hartland Point* was quietly laid aside, we shall never know if her perfomance had improved following the overhaul.

This lack of documentary data on any trials of No. 2039 make conclusions hard to effect. What is recalled with certainty is No. 2039's prolific water consumption, for when working between Lancing and Eastleigh stops had to be made at Chichester and Fareham to replenish the tender. Purely on a mileage basis alone this represents a figure of 87 gall/mile or a 350% increase on what could normally be expected. Much of this was certainly due to the continued breaking of rings; indeed upon routine piston examination most of the rings would be found to be already broken or at the very least cracked. It was never firmly established if this was a design or assembly fault. Consequently when running the front of the loco would be enveloped in steam.

In store outside Brighton Works. It would appear long periods were spent out of use in this way although when she did run it was with any crew that was available and unlike 'Leader' not the responsibility of just a single set of men. The name *Hartland Point* continued to be carried up to the time of eventual withdrawal.

W.H.G. Boot (courtesy N.E. Stead)

Hartland Point in steam at Eastleigh following a trip with carriage underframes from Lancing. Of the three pipes above the cylinders the outer two are for the exhaust and the centre pipe for the steam input from the regulator valve.

S.C. Townroe

Fresh after overhaul in September 1949 and now numbered 32039. Compared with previous views it can be seen that the snifting valves have at some stage been removed from the smokebox casing, possibly when the replacement boiler was fitted. The tender is without any form of ownership and remained as such until condemned along with the engine.

'R.A.' Collection

By February 1951 the end had at last come and a directive was received from Headquarters to move the engine to Eastleigh for assessment. She was found to be unsuitable to make the trip under her own power, probably because of the protracted time spent in store. Accordingly No. 32039 was towed from Brighton by 'C2X' No. 32438. At Eastleigh the final decision was made and after a further brief period in store she was finally cut up.

No. 32039's demise cannot be other than expected. By 1951 she was surplus to requirements, an odd-ball not worthy of maintaining, especially as the design she had pre-determined was already condemned. Her failings as a guinea pig were surely only haste in design for she had at least proved the sleeve valve concept was worthy of further development. It was not through any fault of No. 2039 that 'Leader' failed to accede to her designers wishes. Unfortunately no direct comparative trials or dynamometer car tests were ever carried out with No. 2039 although it is unlikely these could have prolonged her life. She had at least proven the way, even if before 'Leader' ever turned a wheel it was clear there was still a long way to go.

With no useful life left *Hartland Point* was towed to Eastleigh from Brighton on 17.2.51 and photographed a week later on the day she was officially withdrawn. Four weeks later she was again under tow the short distance to the nearby works where she was finally cut up.

Les Elsey

December 1905 – February 1906	Built by Kitson & Co. Given the number '39' by the LBSCR.
October 1908	Steam heating fitted.
June 1913	Named *La France*.
January 1926	Renumbered and renamed by the SR. Now No. 2039 *Hartland Point*.
July 1947	To Brighton Works for conversion as mobile test bed for sleeve valve experiments.
5.11.47	Ex-works from Brighton.
3.12.47	Yard trial at Brighton. Bulleid and Ivatt present.
December 1947	Works visits and trial Brighton–Lewes.
15.12.47	To Lewes in company with No. 2404.
1.1.48	Worked 3-coach set Brighton–Eastbourne.
January 1948	Daily test train Brighton–Groombridge via Lewes. Light engine runs Brighton–Three Bridges. 'K' Class 2-6-0 propelled to Three Bridges and return.
February 1948	Works visit. Trip(s) to Eastleigh. Works visit.
Mar–Jun 1948	Test train on coastway line Brighton to Lewes or Cowden. 3-coach set Brighton to Tunbridge Wells West and return, or same load to Hastings and return.
July–Aug 1948	Works visits?
September 1948	Train of bogie utility vans. To works.
December 1948	Light engine trials to Hastings. Failed at St. Leonards with broken valve rod on 19.12.48.
Jan–Feb 1949	Works. Trials?
14.3.49	First public passenger train Brighton to Redhill and return.
16.3.49	Trial run with 3 coaches Brighton to Redhill, failed at Earlswood.
Apr–Jun 1949	Special to Ashford with Bulleid on footplate. Stock trains Lancing to Eastleigh. Works visits and storage.
14.6.49–3.9.49	Brighton Works. Overhaul.
Sept 1949 – Feb 1951	Stored at Brighton?
17.2.51	Towed from Brighton to Eastleigh.
24.2.51	Withdrawn from Eastleigh.
March 1951	Scrapped at Eastleigh Works.

IN
14.6.49
OUT
3.9.49

1026

32039 Changed Boiler. Steam pipes rem, repd & refitted. Cylinder relief valves rem, repd & refitted. Cylinder cock gear rem, & replaced. Blast pipe rem, cleaned & refitted. Crossheads rem, repd & refitted. Eccentric rods and replaced. Connecting rods & coupling rods, rem, repd & refitted. Engine & Tender uncoupled & recoupled. Blower pipe rem, repd & refitted. Chimney rem & refitted. Inter drawbar rem & refitted. Damper gear rem, repd & refitted. Boilerhead rem, repd & refitted. Steam & vacuum by-pass pipes, rem, repd & refitted. Firehole door, rem, repd & refitted. Pressure gauges (5) rem, repd & refitted. Guard Irons rem, repd & refitted. Horn stays & check plates, rem, repd & refitted. Handrails & pillars, rem, replaced. Injector gear rem, repd & refitted. St. Lubricator rem & replaced. Lagging rem, repd & refitted. Oilboxes, rem, repd & replaced. Reversing gear rem & replaced. Reservoirs, rem, repd & replaced. 4 Splashers rem, repd & refitted. Sandboxes rem & replaced. Sandbox gear & stays rem, repd & refitted. Vacuum cylinder rem, repd & refitted. Wh Brake levers rem, repd & refitted. Whistle gear rem & replaced. Heating & Ashpan Cocks rem & replaced. C.I. runner plate fitted to Smokebox door frame. Stretchers rem & replaced. Swing Chain rem & replaced. Axleboxes rem, repd & refitted. Wheels rem & replaced. Tyres. Springs rem & rem replaced. Spring bolts, rem, repd & refitted. Brake gear rem, repd & refitted & Brake Shafts & brackets rem, repd & refitted & Brake Cylinder rem, repd & replaced. Cocks rem repd & replaced. Clearances LF ⅜" RF ⅜" LB ¾" RB ¾"

Tender No.752. Axleboxes rem, repd & refitted. Brake gear rem, repd & refitted. Brake Shafts & Brackets, rem, repd & refitted. Trailing drawbar rem, repd & refitted. Buffers rem, repd & refitted. Ash pipes rem, repd & refitted. Horn stays rem, repd & refitted. Sanding gear rem, repd & refitted.

		SOUTHERN RAILWAY							

Scheduled Mileage 75,000
Depot Brighton (9)   Class H.1   Engine No. 32039

Reports received of sent to Shops	Engine arrived	Work commenced	Mileage since last Gen. Rep.	Class of Repr.	Boiler No.	Tender No.	Extension of Mileage	Date to Work	Repd. at.
30.4.35	4.6.35	4.6.35	72,790	A	BE1000	752	—	6.7.35	E
4.5.36	8.6.36	8.6.36	16,545	C	"	"	—	4.7.36	"
4.2.38	19.4.38	19.4.38	61,730	A	"1050	"	—	18.5.38	B
	8.11.41	8.11.41	54,291	D	"	"	—	26.11.41	B
22.7.42	14.9.42	18.9.42	61,715	A	"1000	"	—	26.10.42	E
	22.5.45	22.5.45	58,368	C	"	"	—	6.4.45	A
	—	29.12.45	41,920	B	"	"	—	23.2.46	B
	—	14.6.49	18,330	H/Int	931	"	—	3.9.49	B

Withdrawn from Stock as per M.E.'s letter dated 21/2/51. Ref. No.10499/24/2/B. (Our Ref. M.634/2.

Breaking up Order No.958 issued 28/2/51.

Engine record card and last works repair schedule for *Hartland Point*. Only normal repairs are referred to with no comment as to the experimental modifications.

'LEADER' IN DESIGN AND CONSTRUCTION

In describing the design and construction details of the engine it is very tempting to slip into a full engineering résumè of the machine which would be singularly out of place here. Instead it is convenient to divide the locomotive into its two distinct assemblies, the main body unit and the two identical power bogies. This approach then has been taken firstly describing the various major features followed by an illustrative section.

The main body unit consisted of a full length 'fish-belly' frame which supported the boiler and ancillaries together with the fuel bunker and water tanks. All were enclosed within a framed sheet steel casing to form a central fireman's cab, with a driving cab at either end. All three cabs were interconnected by a narrow corridor on the left hand side – assuming No. 1 end (smokebox) to be to the front. To achieve this within the loading gauge and with a boiler diameter of 6ft. 4in. the boiler was offset by 6in. to the right hand side.

The two power bogies were both six-wheeled, chain coupled units. Each was driven by a three cylinder, simple expansion sleeve valve engine and fitted with Bulleid's chain driven variant of the Walschaerts valve gear. All the moving parts were flood lubricated within sheet metal oil baths, this included the spring rigging. As with *Hartland Point* the cylinders were pressure lubricated by separate means.

A study of the photographs showing the locomotive under construction reveals the extensive use of welded steel fabrication. Indeed the whole background for this was to save weight while retaining strength. The effect was to produce 'monocoque' assemblies wherever possible, leaving only those parts that may require periodic replacement as easily serviceable. All other components would only be inspected during times of major works overhaul. With the exception of the wheels, tyres, buffer stocks, axle housings and superheater, the locomotive was largely fabricated or machined from plate, sheet, tube or bar.

Such extensive use of welding was achieved by means of the electric arc which proved to be a highly successful method of marrying steel together. It was a technique unparalleled in the history of steam locomotive construction, where hitherto heavy and expensive machined castings were assembled with either bolts or rivets. Bulleid's Pacific designs had gone some way towards this goal but 'Leader' really did show the way ahead.

Of course an added bonus was that where prototype or one-off experimental work was involved any minor design changes during construction could be affected by the removal of or addition to the affected part by the welder. With the 'Leader' design incorporating so many novel features this facility was used to advantage. Components could also be easily modified where fouls or errors occurred as a side effect of other modifications.

As is referred to in the various photographs, the principles and advantages of the internal combustion engine were followed to an extent in the motion of 'Leader', although the final drive to the wheels was by chain.

Aside from the general appearance of the machine there were a number of features which were such a radical departure from tradition that they warrant a separate mention at this stage. The first concerns the final drive, which as referred to briefly above was via chain. Bulleid's object was to provide for a continuous and even torque, something not possible with a conventional coupling rod, whilst an added bonus was the almost total abolition of any hammer blow. Accordingly the centre crank axle of each bogie was provided with a sprocket on each side, to which chains led to the rear on one side and to the front on the other. Ideally a symmetrical drive on both sides would have been preferred but the constraints of the loading gauge did not allow for this. Therefore the centre and rear axles were fitted with a sprocket on one end only and were completely reversible to allow for exchange if required. Roller bearings were fitted on all axles.

Bulleid's reason for the inclusion of chains probably went back many years to the time he visited an engineering establishment in France where all the machinery was driven in this way. He had learnt at the time that chain drive required little or no maintainance and so obviously saw this as a desirable criteria to incorporate in his steam engines – hence the use of chains in the valve gear of the Pacifics. This time though the idea was taken a stage further. While there were certainly advantages with this system, the unsymmetrical drive caused obvious disadvantages, notably the unbalanced stresses acting upon the crank axle, with a pull from one side on the top and on the opposite side underneath. It was never proven, but this may well have later contributed to the crank axle failure suffered by No. 36001 on test.

The springing of the engine was also unique and besides using a conventional leaf spring, a pair of oil filled dashpots either side of the axle assisted in damping vertical movement. This was without doubt a resounding success and should have given a far better ride than any other steam engine. Unfortunately the unbalanced weight distribution tended to counter any advantages gained and a tendency to find the movement of the axleboxes within the horns rather rigid also negated its success. This in the opinion of S.C. Townroe was another factor likely to have contributed to the crank axle failure.

However, it was with the type of braking on 'Leader' that Bulleid scored an undoubted triumph. So much so that it is a wonder why such a simple principle was not utilised on other engines. As was the custom, 'Leader' was vacuum braked, but instead of a single reservoir which was manually charged by an ejector under the control of the driver, this time there were a number of separate storage tanks. Two of these were fitted at the rear end of each bogie and fed from a pair of larger storage tanks located adjacent to the smokebox. The principle was simple, on a brake application being made the bogie tanks were automatically recharged from the storage tanks, which would themselves automatically bring the ejector into use when the level of vacuum dropped to a pre-determined level. This was similar to the later concept of air-braked systems on modern diesel and electric engines; allied to which the total adhesion and clasp brakes with which the engine was fitted gave the driver confidence in control and braking power hitherto unknown with a steam design.

Left and right hand prefabricated steel box section bogie frames for one bogie and clearly showing the method of welded construction. The three triangular apertures were for access to the laminated suspension springs. The raised edges and lugs had the spring covers secured to them later. At this stage the frames were then ready to be placed in the assembly welding fixture – see next photograph. All the various bogie components then had to be welded into position including cylinders, stretchers, buffer beam etc.

National Railway Museum

A bogie frame assembly in an advanced stage of construction and shown located in the welding fixture. At this instance it is orientated in the upside down position. The frame itself could be rotated through 360 degrees to allow the welders ease of access to any section and was an idea used in Germany during World War II when 'U' boats were made in this way. As shown most of the major sub-assemblies are attached with the cylinders on the right hand side. Years later doubts would be raised as to whether the concentration of heat built up when the cylinder assembly was welded into position did not cause slight distortion to the cylinders themselves and so precipitate some of the problems encountered with the sleeve valves.

National Railway Museum

A three cylinder assembly for one of the 'Leader' bogies. Each cylinder was of 12¼in. bore by 15in. stroke and so was in itself relatively small when judged against conventional locomotive standards. This view is from the rear and shows within the bores the various inlet and outlet ports for the steam. There were 13 of each per bore, the wider ports used for the exhaust. As with the earlier experiments on No. 2039 a mechanite sleeve was later slid into each bore and when in use the whole was enveloped within a full length steam jacket. Invisible in the photograph is a separate connection for the oil pressure lubrication to the sleeves and bores. Similarly the main pipes for steam admission and exhaust to the assembly were to be added later to the top.

National Railway Museum

Sleeve valves slid into position within the cylinders. The lugs onto which the oscillating gear will later be attached can also be seen protruding from the front of each sleeve – note the angles at which the sleeves are shown as reposing were only temporary and were later altered at the time of valve setting. Within each sleeve were a number of slots machined to correspond with the slots within the cylinder casing. Through these the steam was admitted and exhausted from the pistons. Above the left hand buffer was a lifting shackle attached to an eyelet, the former is a temporary affair and would be removed before the locomotive was released for trials. Brighton works, 26.3.49.

Collection of D. Broughton

The valve gear was driven from the centre axle of each bogie and with three inside cylinders on each bogie, the centre crank axle was unusual in that it was therefore fitted with a three throw crank shaft, in some respects similar to the internal combustion engine. This view is from underneath but has been deliberately transposed to make it easier to follow. Of the features visible the three eccentric rods connecting the pistons can be seen and also the morse chain used to drive the separate valve gear crankshaft – this last named item is not visible. The large bar almost central in the view is a support for the crankshaft and the circular shaft behind the valve gear was later removed from view and sealed within the oil bath, intended to require nil maintainance, being not only flood lubricated whenever the engine was in motion but also sealed against the ingress of foreign bodies. Similar again to the principles of the internal combustion engine. Just discernable to the top right of the brake shaft is a small funnel shaped duct. This is for the disposal of smokebox ash and of course similar to the earlier experiments of 1896.

National Railway Museum

Rear view of a part completed bogie. (This is the rear bogie for No. 36001.) The two circular containers at the bottom of the view are vacuum reservoirs with a similar pair on the front bogie. Of particular interest here are the centre mounting pads for the body to sit on the bogie, two are visible along the longitudinal axis, while two more were yet to be added in a horizontal position. Each mounting consisted of a 'Mintex' pad deliberately scored with a number of grooves to act as oil channels. In this way the use of a centre pivot was avoided and was without doubt an unqualified success. The rearmost covering to the oil-bath had yet to be added, in which would be a sealed 18 in. square manhole intended for inspection purposes. A keen eye will observe the Leader-type boiler combine or manifold resting on the bench.

National Railway Museum

A wheel and crank axle set with the axlebox dampers and drive sprocket attached. The axle clearly shows two of the three cranks together with the smaller sprocket for driving the valve gear. The wheels themselves were pressed onto the axles using a 100 ton press. It was later alleged that the cranks' webs had not been supported with the customary wooden packing during this operation. The leading and trailing axles to each bogie were similar but obviously consisted of a plain unit.

National Railway Museum

Crank and plain axles depicted at Brighton after delivery from Eastleigh on 1.10.48. The external sprockets were protected against damage in transit by wooden packing. Note also the centre webs have yet to be machined.

Collection of D. Broughton

No. 1 power bogie nearing completion with the oscillating gear attached to the front of the sleeves. Again the oil bath cover to the front of this has yet to be added. Between the first and second axle is the steam turbine for driving flood lubricating oil pumps. The steps for access to the cab are probably one of the ugliest features of the whole design, yet such a style was required to allow for when the engine stopped on a curve, still permitting the driver to reach the cab with ease. The unsymmetrical drive associated with the engine is also visible and with the chain connecting centre with rear axles. On the opposite side the drive was centre to front.

National Railway Museum

As with the bogies the design of the engine from the frames upwards contained much in the way of innovation. The main frames themselves were of welded steel fabrication and braced through their length by four main stretchers and two end channels. Following the construction of a full size wooden mock up, the first pair of main frames are shown amongst an amount of clutter at Brighton Works on 11.5.48 and before the cross bracing has been added. Supporting each side were no less than 27 vertical gussets.

Collection of D. Broughton

43

The heart of the engine, the boiler and firebox, in the course of construction. All five 'Leader' boilers were built at Eastleigh before being moved to Brighton for incorporation into the engines. This rear view shows the barrel and crown completed with the thermic syphons supporting the crown and running down onto the continuation of the throat plate. The first section of plain sheet for the firebox (dry-side/back) is also in position at the rear. Above on the crown the two water gauges are visible. This view gives a very good impression of the advantage to be gained by the use of the syphons together with their large surface area for heat conduction. Note also that instead of stays in the syphons their place is taken by small cross tubes on the flat areas only. These provided yet further successful areas of heat transference. All this was aimed towards producing a successful steam raising vessel allied to reduced maintainance. As with other components the boiler seam was joined by welding, with the actual joints submitted to X-ray examination as a check for accuracy.

National Railway Museum

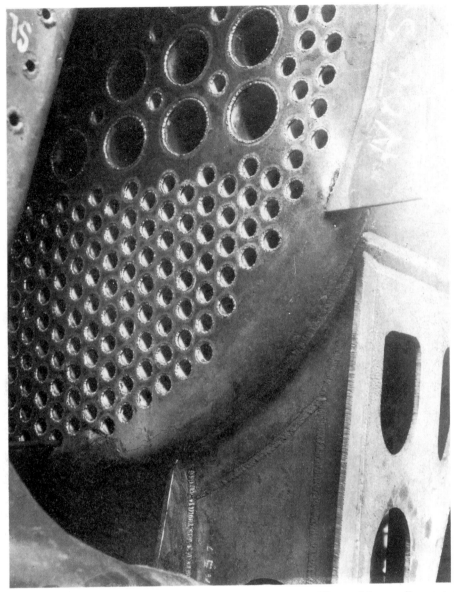

A close up of the throatplate with the tubes welded into position. Three of the small cross tubes in place of stays within the syphons, and referred to in the previous view also, show up well. Tubes were normally placed in position and the ends then expanded using special tools to provide a tight fit. The task of the boilermaker at the steam shed was to deal with any tubes which had worked loose perhaps by vibration and were thus leaking. Again, however, a thankless and time consuming job. As with the Pacifics, which were similarly fitted with welded ends to the tubes, 'Leader' never required such maintainance and this aspect of construction was another success. Altogether there were a total of 283 small or smoke tubes and 36 large superheater tubes giving a heating surface of 2,127 sq.ft. As an aside if a tube did split in service it had to be cut out and was then classed as scrap. These spent tubes were often sold to the staff as clothes posts – look in many of the gardens in Eastleigh even today!

National Railway Museum

The syphons joined to the base of the boiler just ahead of the throatplate and each was provided with a washout plug. Ahead of this the small flange was for the blowdown valve which removed sediment from the boiler water following attention from the the standard T.I.A. water treatment.

Collection of H.A.P. Browne

A 'Leader' boiler on its flat truck after transfer from Eastleigh to Brighton on 6.9.48. The dry sides to the firebox had been added, with the offset firehole door showing up well. The ribbing to the sides of the firebox was intended as additional strength against buckling and in anticipation of the considerable heat that would be generated within. The firebox itself, as first provided allowed for a grate area of 43 sq.ft., with the boiler pressure to Bulleid's standard 280 p.s.i. As with the boiler and smokebox, the firebox sides were lagged externally not only to retain heat but in an effort to reduce the temperature within the firing compartment. During assembly of the boiler within the main body unit a 'mantle shelf' tank 2in. deep was provided around the firebox, which contained water, again with the idea of heat dissipation. Unfortunately in practice the water in this small tank became so hot it raised the temperature of the main water tank and sometimes caused difficulties in getting the injectors to work.

Collection of D. Broughton

Side view of a completed boiler (again at Eastleigh) and incorporating the type of steam manifold visible on the workbench in an earlier view. At this stage the boiler is awaiting testing and has therefore had its various fittings temporarily blanked off. The leading flange for example will later form the connection to the multi-valve poppet-type regulator. Two ross-poppet type safety valves are fitted. Testing the boilers was to 350 p.s.i. under hydraulic means followed by a 290 p.s.i. steam test, both of these conducted outside the main works. An interesting point worth mentioning is that many of the views of the engine at this stage show it in photographers grey, the various parts painted in this hue so as to show up better for the official (and other!) photographers.

'R.A.' Collection

Firebricks for 'Leader' which were used to line the dry sides within the firebox. Each brick had a number cast into it to indicate its position. The various pieces connected as in a jig-saw and were secured by small hooks at the top of each row.

National Railway Museum

Rocking grate below the firebox. This was not physically attached to the boiler assembly and instead the firebox rested on the heat resistant pads to front and rear.

National Railway Museum

The hopper ashpan with the damper doors also just visible – one on either side. Note with this item construction was by a mixture of bolts and welds. The ashpan assembly hung beneath the centre of the engine and was able to discharge without difficulty into a pit without the need for manhandling back through the firehole doors.

National Railway Museum

An unusual view from beneath the main frames which shows the complexity of pipework for the injectors. The actual control spindles connected via a universal joint and ran up towards the fireman's compartment from the centre of the view. At this stage the frames and boiler were supported on a specially built wooden cradle.

National Railway Museum

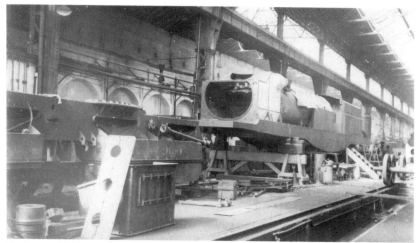

Brighton Works, 26.3.49 with the boiler mounted on the frame. A careful study of the view will reveal the boiler and smokebox offset to the left of the frames to allow for the side corridor. Ahead of the boiler is the smokebox and as this will be hidden by the outer casing its design is purely functional with little in the way of aesthetic considerations. An amount of fibreglass lagging has also been applied. To the right hand side the oblong casing forms the shelf tank, which was located on the extreme side of the corridor. Although it is not referred to as such in official reports this may well have been included in an effort to reduce the uneven weight distribution caused by the offset boiler.

Collection of D. Broughton

The bunker in the course of assembly with the side panel still to be fitted. The coal space is clearly marked by the triangular section, whilst the baffles were intended not only to support the structure but to reduce water surge and are also visible. To the left is the shovel plate and unusually is positioned so that the coal had to be shovelled at 90 degrees to the bunker itself. This is within the centre or firing position of the engine. No. 2 or bunker end driving position would be at the extreme right hand side. This view was taken a few moments prior to an official photograph of the same area, the official photographer visible to the right while his assistant readies himself with a flash light. Coal capacity was 4 imperial tons, and 4000 gallons of water were also carried inclusive of the mantle and shelf tanks.

Collection of D. Broughton

50

Driving cab at No. 1 (smokebox) end showing the well laid out arrangement of controls and instrumentation.

National Railway Museum

A   Pendant type regulator handle
B   Main brake valve
C   Steam reverser control
D   Cylinder cock control
E   Whistle valve lever (Dotted lines indicate the normal position of the hanging lever – removed at the time the view was taken.)
F   Steam heating valve
G   Vacuum release valve
H   Windscreen wiper motor switch

Instruments

I   Reverser positional indicator 'needle'
J   Graduated positional quadrant plate for (I)
K   Boiler steam pressure gauge
L   Steam chest pressure gauge
M   Duplex vacuum brake gauge
N   Steam heating gauge

Electrical

O   Bank of six toggle switches for route indicator lamps
P   Bank of four toggle switches for cab, drawhook and instrument illumination lamps
Q   Reverser control quadrant illumination
R   Main instrument illumination
S   Boiler pressure illumination
T   Cab illumination lamp (Not shown but located above the top left hand frame of the centre window)

Components

U   Corridor viewing mirror
V   Drivers padded swivel seat
W   Centre window catch
X   Lower rollers for roller-sliding door
Y   Left hand drivers door
Z   Windscreen wiper motor (Blade is hidden behind regulator handle)

Adjacent to the centre window catch the whistle valve chain is hanging. A whistle isolating wheel valve was located above the right hand frame of the centre window.

Almost complete and the top body assembly is lowered onto its power bogies. Reversing was via a steam cylinder mounted underneath the body and on one side. Then via a series of shafts and couplings the reversing and cut off adjustments were transmitted equally to each bogie. Contrary to general belief the body sides were not flat but described a 50ft. inward facing curve. At this stage a degree of minor work remained, including covers to the springs, drive chains and oscillating gear and connection of the various steam pipes.

National Railway Museum

15.6.49, just one week to go and this time the painters are at work giving the engine its undercoat of black.

Collection of D. Broughton

Until now the general belief has been that 'Leader' always ran in an overall grey livery and yet here are two views taken on 20 & 21.6.49, never previously seen which should demolish such tradition. Evidently the overall black was only carried within the works and when the engine ventured out on the first trials this had been replaced by grey. In the opinion of the present writer this was a pity as lined out she would have been very smart. Certainly at that time, Brighton Works were expected to produce the latest batch of West Country engines, also in black, but in the event green was used for those engines. Drawgear was attached to the bogies themselves and a single whistle located above the windows at either end. These were independently operated.

Both collection of D. Broughton

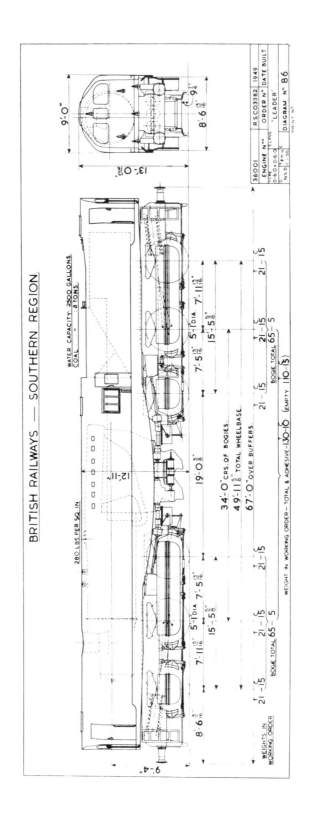

Side elevation of complete engine

VACUUM BRAKE SYSTEM INCORPORATING AUTOMATIC CONTROL OF
EJECTOR FOR STEAM LOCOMOTIVE WITH CAB AT BOTH ENDS

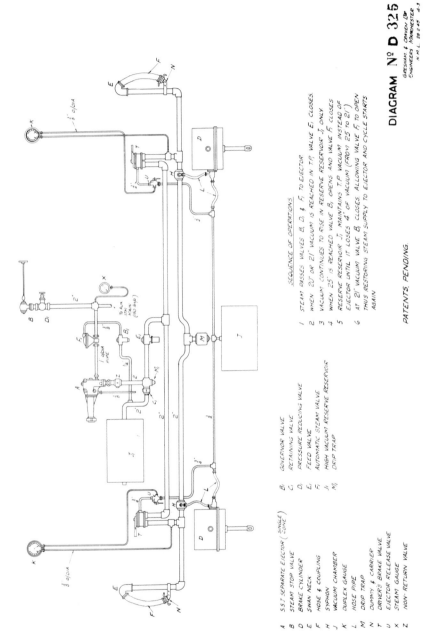

A   S.S.T SEPARATE EJECTOR (SINGLE CONE)
B   STEAM STOP VALVE
D   BRAKE CYLINDER
E   SWAN NECK
F   HOSE & COUPLING
H   SYPHON
J   VACUUM CHAMBER
K   DUPLEX GAUGE
L   HOSE PIPE
M   DRIP TRAP
N   DUMMY & CARRIER
T   DRIVER'S BRAKE VALVE
U   EJECTOR RELEASE VALVE
X   STEAM GAUGE
Z   NON-RETURN VALVE

B₁   GOVERNOR VALVE
C₁   RETAINING VALVE
D₁   PRESSURE REDUCING VALVE
E₁   FEED VALVE
F₁   AUTOMATIC STEAM VALVE
J₁   HIGH VACUUM RESERVE RESERVOIR
M₁   DRIP TRAP

SEQUENCE OF OPERATIONS

1   STEAM PASSES VALVES B, D, & F, TO EJECTOR
2   WHEN 20" OR 21" VACUUM IS REACHED IN T.P. VALVE E₁ CLOSES.
3   VACUUM CONTINUES TO RISE IN RESERVE RESERVOIR J₁ ONLY
4   WHEN 25" IS REACHED VALVE B₁ OPENS AND VALVE F₁ CLOSES
5   RESERVE RESERVOIR J₁ MAINTAINS T.P VACUUM INSTEAD OF
     EJECTOR UNTIL IT LOSES 4" OF VACUUM (FROM 25 TO 21")
6   AT 21" VACUUM VALVE B₁ CLOSES ALLOWING VALVE F₁ TO OPEN
     THUS RESTORING STEAM SUPPLY TO EJECTOR AND CYCLE STARTS
     AGAIN

PATENTS PENDING.

DIAGRAM Nº D 325

GRESHAM & CRAVEN LTD
ENGINEERS MANCHESTER
N.M.L. 28 2 45   4-3

Schematic diagram of braking system

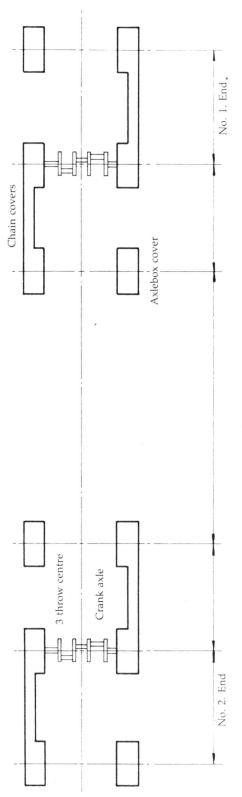

Chain covers

Axlebox cover

No. 1. End.

3 throw centre

Crank axle

No. 2. End

Drawing of unsymmetrical drive

'LEADER' ON TEST

Part One – The runs from Brighton

Following the satisfactory completion of the requisite stationary tests within Brighton Works, the first 'Leader' was finally ready for trials on 21 June 1949. On that morning it was hauled out into the public gaze alongside the main line by the Brighton Works shunter.

It was planned to stage the first running trial on the following day, but fate was to show its hand even at this early stage, for after running light the short distance from the works to the station, the engine failed to reverse and had to be towed back into the works for attention. Upon examination it was found that the valve operating rod to the middle sleeve on No.1 bogie was broken whilst the oscillating gear lever of the same cylinder was bent. Besides the necessary repairs the relevant parts on both bogies were strengthened.

Therefore it was not until 25 June that the delayed first trip was made. A run to Oxted via Groombridge and Lewes. As before with No. 2039 the operating authorities were taking no chances with 'Leader' and so the run was in tandem to a small tank engine. Mechanically there were no problems, even the 1 in 60 climb out of Lewes was accomplished with ease. But at Groombridge an obscure difficulty loomed, for on stopping to take on water it was found that the water column was too low to reach the high filling point on 'Leader'; so recourse had to be made to a small hose connected to a tap in the porters office! Evidently in the haste surrounding the design no one had given a thought to the fact that the water columns on the central division of the Southern were intended for engines with low filling points and so through no fault of the engine the test was abandoned and a return made to Brighton.

The following day, 26.6.49, a more successful run was made, this time along the coast line from Brighton through Chichester to Fareham and Eastleigh, in company with 'K' class mogul No. 32343.

This particular trip may well have been partly a publicity exercise aimed at the hierarchy of the Railway Executive, for No. 36001 was to remain at Eastleigh for three days during which time she was visited by a number of senior officials. In addition the engine number was painted midway along both sides and the standard 'cycling lion' BR emblem applied. Overall though the livery was still grey. In this state the locomotive was recorded by the official photographer. No attempt was made to weigh the engine and instead she was steamed for a return to Brighton, this time alone, on 29.6.49. Unfortunately the trip was not as successful as the outward run, for en route a considerable amount of knocking was heard from No. 1 bogie allied to which the exhaust was distinctly 'off-beat'.

At Brighton Works the same middle valve rod as before was found fractured, with a similar defect on the adjacent left hand rod. Examination of the associated sleeve valves also found these damaged, the centre one broken in four places and that on the left showing signs of seizure.

Brighton Station, 21.6.49. 'Leader' just emerged from the works and impatiently blows off excess steam in anticipation of its first trial run.

Collection of D. Broughton

22.6.49 and the first failure after 'Leader' refused to reverse at Brighton Station. This is the reversing gear of the engine, actuated by a small steam cylinder and intended to impart the same 'cut-off' to both bogies simultaneously.

Collection of D. Broughton

For the delayed initial trip an 'E4' tank was coupled to 'Leader' for the first run to Falmer and Groombridge. The pair are seen outside Brighton works prior to the trip. Sharp eyed readers will note no cast numberplate had as yet been fitted to No. 36001.

Collection of D. Broughton

After the embarassing experience of the first run, a crude but effective means was devised for ensuring that adequate supplies of water could be taken. This consisted of a copper chute attached to a leather bag which effectively extended the reach of the low water columns on the central division. (On the later tests from Eastleigh no such problems were encountered.) A slight disadvantage was that water tended to spray in all directions when the extension was in use! The assembly was carried on the engine for the duration of the time it was based at Brighton and here is seen in use during a pause in testing at Oxted. A useful comparison can be drawn with the height of the locomotive tender on the opposite platform.

H.W. Attwell

Bulleid felt the cause may well have been due to insufficient allowance for expansion of the sleeves within the cylinders and so all three sleeves were reduced in diameter by 0.0018in. but only on No.1 bogie.

The repairs meant the engine was out of service until 7.7.49 when light engine tests resumed. Two runs were made to Falmer and Groombridge and with a repeat working the following day. On 11 July the engine would seem to have been scheduled for a test but this was cancelled at the last moment and instead the same runs as before were made the following day, 12 July.

Two days later on the morning of 14 July, a further run was made, again light engine to Crowborough. Both Bulleid and Granshaw, the Brighton Works Manager were on the engine, which performed the task set without difficulty. During the afternoon a repeat was again attempted but this time without the designer present. At Barcombe Mills however, north of Lewes the engine failed, with all three valve rods from No. 1 bogie fractured, which also caused damage to various ancillary components. The result was a tow back to Brighton, with only 360 miles 'on the clock' from new.

Not surprisingly there was now a nine day interlude when in addition to the required repairs a number of modifications to the valve gear were undertaken. Externally too there were changes, with the grey sides lined out as panels painted in red and black.

With repairs effected 'Leader' was steamed again on 23 July running light to Crowborough without incident. The following day the destination was Seaford and again light engine. Two runs were planned to each location. But approaching Seaford on the second trip the valve gear on No. 1 bogie again developed trouble and a slow return was therefore made to Brighton. It transpired that at the time of the breakdown the

'Leader's' first visit to Eastleigh and being shunted into the Works by a grimy 'D15' No. 464. No. 36001 is shown on its blind side and is as yet un-numbered. No. 1, smokebox end is to the right. Just past the mid-way point along the casing roof are a number of small openings intended as vents to the firemans compartment. A number of others existed on the opposite side. A sliding vent in the centre of the cab roof was also located in each cab. Besides the engine the superb pole route is worthy of a second glance.

W. Gilburt

Official view of No. 1 end taken outside Eastleigh Works. Between the body unit and bogies the curved cover is the end of the oil bath behind which is the reciprocating mechanism for the sleeve valves.

National Railway Museum

engine was running in full forward gear (about 75% cut off) and at a rather higher speed than usual – this was the equivalent of running a motor car hard in first gear. But even so there must have been many puzzled faces in the works, had not the engine just run 100 miles without defect? Yet now it was the right hand valve rod that was broken along with the associated sleeve.

Why were there these continuous failures and why always the same components on the same bogie? Hindsight may provide a possible solution. Evidently whilst the engine was under construction in the works the completed No. 1 bogie was supported on blocks and supplied with steam for a static test. It ran perfectly sweetly on only an 8 p.s.i. supply, but then on instructions from a senior officer the complete assembly was put into reverse while still running forward causing considerable damage to a number of components. Most were just straightened out as best as possible afterwards.

Following repairs, which included relining both sides and part of the back of the firebox, the engine was again steamed on 12.8.49. (The reference to repairs to the firebox is interesting as at this stage no defects concerning this item are recorded in official minutes.) This was the start of a six day series of light engine tests to Crowborough – seven trips, Seaford and Lewes. The runs were marred by one failure, at Seaford on 15 August, when a pin fell out of the valve gear, but rapid repairs were made to enable the trials to continue. Even allowing for this incident the series were the most successful so far, the engine proving to be both free steaming and free running and with speeds up to 70 mph attained with ease. A note in official records against the runs relates, '. . . difficulties with the firebox lining which has a tendency to fall out of position . . . .' and '. . . control of the regulator and reverser erratic.' Perhaps a similar situation as with the previous reference to firebox repairs.

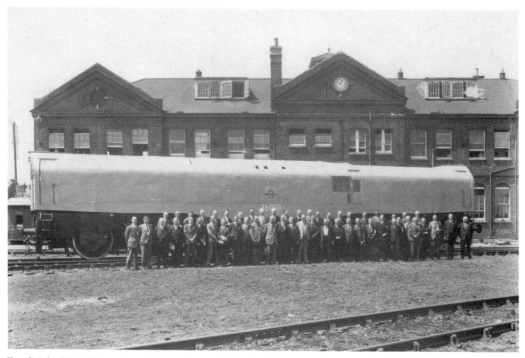

Eastleigh 28.6.49 and an inspection of 'Leader' by members of the Railway Executive and Association of Locomotive Engineers. The engine was in steam and moved up and down the yard for demonstration. Beneath the roof ventilators the 'cycling lion' BR emblem and engine number have now been applied. This together with a further coat of 'works grey' was applied in the open air of the works yard.

Collection of J. Bell

The problems with the regulator were in maintaining the desired pressure within the steam chest, also the reverser was difficult to 'notch up' (change gear).

It was inevitable that following what had been a modicum of success a load haulage trial would next be attempted. So on 18.8.49 a train of ten bogie vehicles, totalling some 248 tons was assembled in Brighton yard, which No. 36001 was set to haul to Eastleigh.

Bulleid was at this time absent from the scene, on holiday with fellow members of the Association of Railway Locomotive Engineers in Perthshire. That is not to say he was out of touch, for a series of progress telegrams were sent to his holiday hotel by Granshaw.

The actual run to Eastleigh referred to above is particularly interesting, as conflicting reports exist as to its success. Granshaw in a telegram to Bulleid reported all was well; yet according to official records a portion of the firebox lining collapsed en route which necessitated repairs upon arrival at Eastleigh. The open ash duct in the smokebox was also welded shut at the same time after which all smokebox cleaning had to be undertaken by manual means.

At Eastleigh the opportunity was taken to weigh the engine on the works weigh table with fearful results! Instead of the 110 tons in working order of its design and as estimated from calculations during construction, the true weight turned out to be 130½ tons. The comments which must have been made by the hierarchy are not recorded – perhaps it is just as well!

No. 36001 was worked back light to Brighton on 20 August, but failed once more, this time at Barnham. Again the cause was due to breakage of the sleeve valve on No. 1 bogie, the firebox lining also refused to stay in place.

Stationary at Lewes on 17.8.49 with a fair gathering of interested onlookers. The not inconsiderable amount of black smoke would indicate the fire was built up whilst the engine was standing. Any enquiry as to the machine by a member of the public was greeted with the response that all was well.

Collection of H.C. Casserley

Receiving attention inside Brighton Works in August 1949 and with the oil bath cover of the oscillating gear removed on No. 1 bogie. A minor point is that the engine now had its lining out applied on top of the grey livery while the painted number has been removed from the centre of the sides to near the cab doors.

Collection of D. Broughton

Another failure, this time at Barnham on 20.8.49 when returning to Brighton from Eastleigh. On this occasion there was a broken sleeve on No. 1 bogie along with difficulties with the firebox lining.

W.N.J. Jackson

Back at Brighton another nine days were spent out of service enabling repairs and modificatons to take place. These included reducing the maximum cut-off from 75–65%, a spark arrester was supposedly fitted at this point.

Trials recommenced on 30.8.49 the engine running light to Crowborough. These continued until 2 September and were marred only once by a single firebrick coming loose. (Accordingly, with confidence again restored, on 5.9.49 the most ambitious test to date was set.) No. 36001 was to haul eight bogie vehicles totalling 260 tons to Victoria via Oxted. This was of course only slightly heavier than that previously taken to Eastleigh but unfortunately the run was terminated at Oxted as there were difficulties in maintaining the required steam pressure, despite a stop for a 'blow-up' at Dormans. The return from Oxted was light engine.

Brighton were of the opinion that the spark arrester may have been partly to blame for the difficulties encountered so it was removed, the same trial was then rearranged for 8.9.49. However, fate was to determine that London would never witness a 'Leader' in steam, for once again the test was terminated at Oxted for exactly the same reasons as before. This it should be said was not due to any fault on the part of the driver and fireman who had both manfully struggled with their tasks in an attempt to retain sufficient boiler pressure. Once more then it returned light to Brighton.

A successful trip to London would no doubt have been an ego-boosting exercise for the design, although, against the available evidence the decision to curtail the trial was the only one possible. It was one thing to disrupt the sporadic service on the relatively

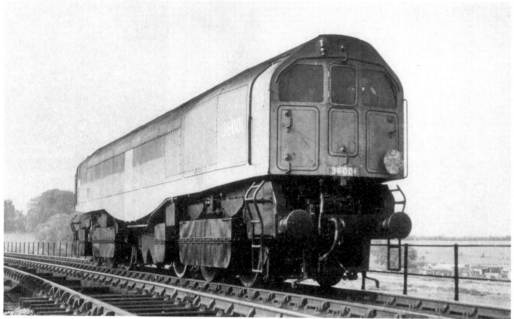

Running light near Lewes following repairs. To provide slightly easier access to the front of the valves the flexible pipe for the steam heating to a following train had been removed although it was later replaced. For the same reason the oil bath cover is missing and while this allowed the operation of the motion to be observed with the engine running – after removal of sections of the floor – a side effect was that dirt and grit could also enter. The very items the cover and oil bath were intended to keep out. We shall never know if such ingress of foreign bodies precipitated any of the valve failures.

C.C.B. Herbert

Dormans, September 1949 and time for a 'blow-up' on the return to Brighton from Oxted after an abortive attempt to reach Victoria. 'Leader' had failed to surmount the 1 in 210 climb to the station with a trailing load of 260 tons. Included with the group on the platform is W.H. 'Joe' Hutchinson who had so much to do with the engine from its inception on the drawing board.

H.W. Attwell

The end of the platform at Brighton afforded a good view of the running shed. 'Leader' framed between 'Q1' No. 33040 and diesel shunter DS1173 and perhaps awaiting a test run.

Collection of D. Broughton

quiet route through Oxted, but the resulting hold-ups caused by a failure nearer London would have been chaotic.

Investigation now centred on two problems, poor steaming and the instability of the firebox lining. Regarding the former, it was felt that the fault lay with the front end design and so the size of the chokes were altered within the multiple jet blast pipe. At the same time a new and, it was hoped, more resilient type of firebrick lining was fitted.

Trials recommenced on 16.9.49, with No. 36001 twice taking empty coaching stock to Crowborough and return. There were no problems with either the firebox or valve gear this time but still the steaming difficulties persisted. After a further modification to the blast pipe a repeat run was made three days later but once more with the same difficulties.

Following yet another modification to the blast pipe the engine was again set to haul an empty stock train to Crowborough. However, at Uckfield it was the turn of the valve gear to play up again, with a fracture of the middle sleeve on No. 1 bogie at the point where the extending 'ears' were attached to the oscillating gear. With the appropriate gear dismantled by the fitter who accompanied the engine on every trial an ignominious return was made to Brighton.

Two days, 21/22 September were spent in the works under repair, during which time besides making good the obvious repairs, two very interesting modifications were carried out. The first involved the removal of the sleeve oscillating gear from No. 1 bogie and steel valve guides replaced the mechanite liners. How much of this can be credited to Bulleid is uncertain for as time went on more and more control was being exercised from the Railway Executive. Bulleid even had to get permission from this organisation to travel on his own engine! Another repair was to the lower firebricks, some of which were found to be badly worn and reported 'patched' as needed.

In disgrace at Uckfield on 20.9.49. As well as the crew a fitter was present throughout the trials, whilst it was also common for a number of other observers to be carried. The engine had failed with a broken sleeve valve.

H.W. Attwell

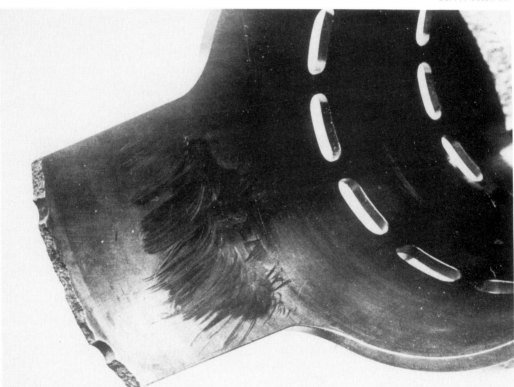

A failed sleeve valve on 'Leader', possibly as a result of the incident at Uckfield, although to be fair there were several such occurances. The broken casting should have continued on to form the lugs to which the oscillating gear was attached. The score marks both within the sleeve and at the end are likely to have been caused by the sticking of the valve during its movement. After a number of similar failures the oscillating gear was eventually removed from both bogies.

National Railway Museum

The changes were tested by running light to Crowborough from 23 to 25 September. A total of five round trips amounting to some 235 miles. Other than slight attention to the firebricks after the last journey no problems were encountered. Accordingly further runs with load haulage were commenced, these started on 27.9.49 and involved 5 bogie vehicles weighing 150 tons to either Crowborough, Lewes or Oxted. The runs continued until the last day of the month by which time 447 miles had been covered with no mechanical difficulties reported, although steaming was once again erratic.

A repeat series was arranged, commencing on 3.10.49, but in addition to the poor steaming the firebox brickwork was found to be in poor condition after the last run. Also a new problem had emerged, for on the first day both chains on the oil circulating pump came off, and on the second day of the trials the governer valve of the same pump was suspect. Both these were potentially serious failures, for without a guarantee of adequate lubrication the likelihood of seizure increased.

Repairs were again undertaken at Brighton, the firebricks being replaced by a cast iron type, possibly the first time such items had been used in a railway environment.

Tests resumed on 9.10.49 with No. 36001 set to take 150 tons to Groombridge. At Crowborough, however, the trial was halted, the cast iron firebricks having melted into the fire on one side and were threatening to do the same on the opposite side. This caused the metal side sheet of the firebox to become red hot, making it impossible to continue if only for the sake of the firemen. Ironically, despite all this radiant heat percolating around the interior of the engine there had still been problems with poor steaming! After allowing matters to cool off sufficiently the return to Brighton was minus a train.

This last failure is of special interest because of the questions it raised. Firstly, the use of cast iron firebricks is in itself open to question, especially as the heat needed to raise the temperature enough to melt cast iron indicated a terrific draw on the fire. The fault

Driver Bill Long (left), Fireman Ted Forder (centre) and a Brighton fitter at Crowborough 9.10.49 the occasion of the melted fire bricks. All three were no doubt glad to escape from the torrid interior of the engine on that occasion. Apart from the fitter carried on every trip, there was one run when no less than 18 others were on board the engine, no doubt causing conditions to become a bit cramped. The fitters were not provided with any special tools and so the amount of repairs undertaken en route was restricted. The three men, together with Mr Attwell, who was also on board, were waiting for the firebox sides to cool down before returning to Brighton. Unfortunately this was not the first failure of the refractory bricks and on every occasion this occurred the dry sides of the firebox would distort a little more with the heat and meant the replacement bricks were even more likely to fall down.

H.W. Attwell

Brighton shed and the engine being made ready for a day's testing. Bill Long is in the driver's cab and Ted Forder leaning from the fireman's window. Ted was the fireman on all the runs from Brighton and in conversation with Les Warnett is reported as holding very different views on the engine compared with many. He recounts the troubles with overheating in the centre compartment were greatly exaggerated, the engine cooler than a 'West Country' on a summers day and far preferable. Stories of him having to visit his G.P. after firing the engine are totally unfounded. Likewise he had no objections to working No. 36001 with No. 1 end leading and indeed this was often necessary due to the destinations chosen. The acceleration and braking were described as 'excellent' and certainly equal to the electric units he has driven since. Raising steam too was simple, the ability of the boiler to generate steam in a short space of time was better than a Brighton 'Terrier'.

W.N.J. Jackson

was clearly apparent even then, the steam that was being produced was not being used to best effect. Yet it would appear little attempt was made to rectify what was beginning to show up as a serious design defect. However, before apportioning blame it may well have been that any attempt at a redesign would have possibly brought permanent condemnation from the Railway Executive, so it became a question of attempting to prove the locomotive as sufficiently viable as it stood. Perhaps they felt the chance for rebuilding where necessary would come later. These conclusions are born out following Riddles memorandum of March 1950 (See Appendix G).

The firebox was now relined with conventional material. A new design of brick some 3½in. thick being used. Larger holding hooks were also added.

More tests began on 22.10.49, continuing until the 24th. As before 150 tons was taken to the same destinations. The first two days were successful enough but on the last day the middle sleeve from No. 2 bogie broke while running near Lewes. Examination showed the failure was probably due to fatigue affecting the sleeve 'ears' and so the same modifications that had earlier been undertaken on No. 1 bogie were made, this included the removal of the oscillating gear.

Road runs recommenced on 29.10.49 and at last it looked as if success was within

The creations of Bulleid and Riddles side by side outside Brighton. With the removal of the oil bath cover and gear from the front bogie 'Leader' presents a decidedly naked appearance.

Collection of D. Broughton

reach; for between this date and 16.12.49 no less than 27 days were utilised for test runs, all but three attached to a trailing load. There was even a nine day period in November (although not consecutive days), when an aggregate of 100 miles daily was successfully undertaken and on each occasion again with a trailing load.

The loads hauled varied and included either a five or eight coach empty train of between 153 and 255 tons. A number of defects were reported including broken valve rods and circlips. (Full details of the tests are given in the chronology at the end of this chapter.)

As with previous runs with No. 2039, most of the tests involving No. 36001 commenced from Brighton station. The traffic department providing whatever vehicles they had available to the approximate tonnage stipulated. This accounts for the variance experienced in the daily loadings.

But even if the prototype was perhaps beginning to justify its design, back at Brighton works there was considerable gloom. For BR Headquarters were closely in touch with the progress of the trials and consequently aware of the numerous failures that had occurred earlier. Accordingly a directive was issued on 19.11.49 that work was to cease on the other 'Leader' engines then under construction. This was especially unfortunate for No. 36002 as she was only two days away from completion. Indeed had it not been for the amount of works time her elder sister had spent receiving attention No. 36002 would already have been under test.

It was intended to commence a further series of runs on 14.12.49 but the operating department advised the works that they were unable to supply either the stock or men owing to the build up of the peak holiday season. 'Leader's' last run of the year was on

Running between Brighton and Lewes during November 1949, the headcode was one applicable to trains destined for the Oxted line. This was perhaps the 'best side' of the engine, the windows and door to the fireman's compartment breaking up the plainness of the opposite side. A set of steps afforded access to this centre compartment after which there was a step down into a slight well which formed the floor.

Times Newspapers Ltd

On test 22.11.49, the engine was by now decidedly grubby in appearance. The modifications that had been carried out to the blastpipe were by this time sufficient to promote reasonable steaming and reduce the amount of fire throwing from the chimney. Unfortunately a side effect was a tendency for the fire to creep backwards and lick around the firehole door.

British Railways

No. 1 end leading near Lewes, with the elbow and arm of an unknown individual protruding from the firemans compartment. Temperatures of 122° F were recorded at the window of the centre compartment which allied to the ever present condensation helped give the engine its nickname, 'The Chinese Laundry'. This was not a particularly excessive reading for the engine as other parts, notably the passage alongside the boiler and No. 1 end cab were reputedly hotter – the latter because of the proximity of the smokebox door. The 122° however was considered a fair average.

Times Newspapers Ltd

16 December when she was worked light to Eastleigh again for weighing, she returned the same day. The engine then re-entered the works where it was to remain until 26.1.50. (A record of the weighings of the engine is given in Appendix D.)

So why the period of store for so long after the holiday period, especially when the tests were at last going well? Certainly this was not now due to staff or stock shortage. Instead the answer to this probably lies in the now generally known true weight of the engine. The Chief Civil Engineers department had been made aware of the figures and were understandably perturbed by its possible effect upon both track and bridges. Such concern heightened over the side to side weight variance. Brighton works thus spent time attempting to produce a more stable balance which included two complete changes of springs. A number of other modifications unconnected with the weight problem were also carried out and included work to the brakes, valve gear, lubricators and whistle. Moving ahead in time it was to transpire that the difficulties with the firebox lining had at last been overcome, although to remedy this 9in. wide firebricks were fitted to the lower course. This effectively reduced the grate area from 43 to 25.5 sq.ft., only 5 sq.ft. larger than an M7 tank.

Eight vehicles equal to approximately 250 tons being taken up the 1 in 88 of Falmer Bank near Brighton on the morning of 4.12.49, evidently with consummate ease. The hill climbing abilities of 'Leader' are remembered as considerable, although this was an aspect never fully recounted in official reports. On one particular occasion the 4¾ miles from Buxted to Crowborough were covered in 4½ min, exactly half the scheduled time. Neither was this a unique example, for the same times were repeated the following day. Unfortunately on both occasions the trailing load is not recorded. Such efforts on behalf of both engine and crew were often at the behest of the observers carried. Bulleid himself perhaps saying ' . . . come on, let us get to the top as quick as possible, then if anything is going to fail we will will find out what and why'. Ironically on such occasions failures were rare, although the unexpected demands for steam meant pressure would perhaps fall to only 120 p.s.i. Bulleid is also recalled as being particularly generous on the occasions he travelled and regularly gave the crew £1 between them after every run. Other officials too are recalled for their generosity, one man sharing bars of chocolate with the driver and fireman at a time when such luxury was difficult to obtain.

W.N.J. Jackson

Following this period in store, No. 36001 was steamed on 27.1.50 for a light engine trial to Tunbridge Wells after which further spring adjustments and weighings, this time at Brighton, took place. A few days later on 2.2.50 she ran light to Eastleigh and was again weighed.

The sphere of activity now moves away from the engine itself and instead to the Railway Executive. Robert Riddles, C.M.E. for the whole of BR was understandably concerned over the length of time already undertaken on trials together with the erratic behaviour of the engine. At his request R.G. Jarvis from Brighton prepared a detailed report on progress to date;

LEADER CLASS LOCOMOTIVE

'I have been asked by Mr. Warder (the new Mechanical & Electrical Engineer of the Southern Region) to express my views on this experiment as the Regional Chief Technical Assistant responsible for design. No personal criticism is inferred in the remarks which follow, and the views expressed represent my views which may well be at variance with those of the designers of the locomotive, on the basis that if doctors can differ so may engineers.

The design has certain attractive features, it has many problems to solve, and it has some fundamental defects. That the locomotive could be made to work I have no doubt, but a great deal of experimental work will be necessary. It all depends upon how much money can be permitted for the modifications which will entail virtually a complete re-arrangement.'

The main disadvantages were then listed as follows;

1. The weight will restrict route availaility.
2. The enclosure and lubrication of engines, axleboxes and springs is very unsatisfactory.
3. The increased steam chest volume and port areas and the reduced clearance volumes, may only have a minimal effect on thermal efficiency.
4. Replacement of firebox water-legs by firebricks is not successful.

He continued;

'The disappointing progress made with the locomotive to date is to a much greater extent attributable to the detail design than to the broad conception.'

Continuing on the same theme the following changes were then listed as essential if the locomotive was to be made serviceable;

1. Self aligning bearings are essential.
2. Changes will have to be made to the fireman's compartment, this being very unsatisfactory and dangerous in the event of a blow back upon entering a tunnel.
3. Development work is required to alleviate the problems with the sleeve valve.
4. If it were possible smaller wheels would be deemed preferable.'

Shortly afterwards on 24.3.50 Riddles submitted his own report to the Railway Executive in which he summarised the findings to date as well as putting forward his own recommendations;

'. . . . it has not so far been possible to release this locomotive for revenue earning service.

In view of the special character of this locomotive and to ensure continuity in the work necessary to overcome the difficulties which were experienced, an invitation was extended to Mr. Bulleid, prior to his retirement in September 1949, to remain closely in touch with the developments necessary and supervise any alterations required to ensure that the locomotive should become successful. It was originally thought that 3 months would be sufficient for this work to be completed but in the light of later experience the arrangement with Mr. Bulleid was continued a further 3 months until the end of March this year.

Mr. Bulleid has now intimated his desire to be released from his obligations in this respect and has submitted a memorandum on the subject of the locomotive.' (See Appendix F)

Riddles then dealt with a number of other matters and costings before continuing;

'In view of the unsatisfactory weight distribution and reports of track spreading allegedly due to this locomotive (these were never proven – KJR), trial runs were recently discontinued. Steps are being taken which it is hoped will improve the weight distribution sufficiently to permit a resumption of trial runs, probably at restricted speeds and with a limited amount of coal and water on board. Although the radius of action of the locomotive will be limited by the restrictions on the amount of coal and water carried which it may be necessary to impose, further trial runs will enable proof of performance of the firebox lining and valve mechanism, as already modified, to be obtained. Dynamometer car tests with suitable loads will be conducted to obtain data on coal and water consumption in relation to work done. If the dynamometer car tests do in fact reveal that substantially less fuel and water are required per unit of work done compared with the normal locomotive, consideration will be given to carrying out the further modifications necessary before the locomotive can hope to fulfil its designers expectations.'

Riddles had thus made no attempt to gloss over the failings that had already occurred. Indeed there were a number of members of the Railway Exectutive who were in favour of curtailing the project even at that point. So the emphasis once more returns to Brighton and No. 36001, with everything still at stake and yet with the odds already stacked against success.

Bulleid's feelings upon hearing of this news are not recorded, ensconsed as he was in a new position as C.M.E. of the Irish Railway system. Brighton Works however had been instructed to press ahead with the trials and modifications and so began a number of changes which included the oil supply to the pedestal guides. As a result the riding qualities improved dramatically, the previous harshness now giving way to a smoothness more akin to a passenger carriage.

Leaving Brighton on another test. The high angle of the photograph just shows the opening for the coal bunker at No. 2 end. In the right background are a number of other engines including *Hartland Point*. On one occasion when the Chief Locomotive Tester was travelling alone in the rear cab, two loud cracks were heard which were immediately taken to indicate another sleeve valve failure. It transpired to be nothing more serious than the engine having run over two detonators.

Collection of D. Broughton

In store at Brighton during the winter of 1949/50, with the lower half of the oil bath covers removed from the axles at No. 1 end. Due to the weight of the engine, speed on the later trials was restricted to 50 mph, with a maximum of 3 tons of coal and 2600 gallons of water on board. By this time a number of modifications had been made to the engine, one of the more recent being the sealing off of the pressure relief valves on the cylinders. This action was somewhat drastic for all that was really required was some stronger springs.

W.N.J. Jackson

Elsewhere the Southern Region M. & E.E's department had been instructed to prepare for the dynamometer car trials. Originally these were to have been from Brighton but with the C.C.E. now aware of the true axle weight of the engine which verged on 25 tons (This was the maximum side to side axle weight and not the equal measurement.) he promptly banned any further test running on the Central Section. Bulleid was also alledged to have said at one time '. . . send it to Eastleigh, they will get it going . . .', and it was indeed Eastleigh that was chosen for the trials. No. 36001 steaming away from Brighton for the last time on 13.4.50, some no doubt glad to see it go.

CHRONOLOGY

Trial running from Brighton. 22.6.49–2.2.50.

*	22. 6.49	Initial trial trip
	25. 6.49	Light with E4 tank to Falmer and Groombridge.
	26. 6.49	Light with K class 2-6-0 to Eastleigh.
*	29. 6.49	Light engine Eastleigh to Brighton.
	7. 7.49	Light engine to Falmer and Crowborough.
	8. 7.49	Light engine to Falmer and Crowborough.
	12. 7.49	Light engine to Falmer and Crowborough.
*	14. 7.49	Light to Crowborough, twice.
	23. 7.49	Light to Crowborough.
*	24. 7.49	Light to Seaford.
*	12. 8.49	Light to Crowborough, Seaford and Lewes.
	13. 8.49	Light to Crowborough, Seaford and Lewes.
*	14. 8.49	Light to Crowborough, Seaford and Lewes.
*	15. 8.49	Light to Crowborough, Seaford and Lewes.
*	16. 8.49	Light to Crowborough, Seaford and Lewes.
*	17. 8.49	Light to Crowborough, Seaford and Lewes.
*	18. 8.49	Trial to Eastleigh with 248 tons.
*	20. 8.49	Light Eastleigh to Brighton.

	30. 8.49	Light to Crowborough.
	31. 8.49	Light to Crowborough.
	1. 9.49	Light to Crowborough.
*	2. 9.49	Light to Crowborough.
*	5. 9.49	Intended trial to Victoria with 260 tons.
*	8. 9.49	Intended trial to Victoria with 260 tons.
*	16. 9.49	Trail to Crowborough. Load between 180 and 271 tons.
*	19. 9.49	Trail to Crowborough. Load between 180 and 271 tons.
*	20. 9.49	Trail to Crowborough. Load between 180 and 271 tons.
	23. 9.49	Light to Crowborough.
	24. 9.49	Light to Crowborough.
*	25. 9.49	Light to Crowborough.
*	27. 9.49	Trials to Oxted, Crowborough and Lewes. Load 150 tons.
*	28. 9.49	Trials to Oxted, Crowborough and Lewes. Load 150 tons.
*	29. 9.49	Trials to Oxted, Crowborough and Lewes. Load 150 tons.
*	30. 9.49	Trials to Oxted, Crowborough and Lewes. Load 150 tons.
*	3.10.49	Trials to Crowborough. Load 150 tons.
*	4.10.49	Trials to Crowborough. Load 150 tons.
*	9.10.49	Trials to Crowborough. Load 150 tons.
	22.10.49	Trials to Oxted and Crowborough. Load 150 tons.
	23.10.49	Trials to Oxted and Crowborough. Load 150 tons.
*	24.10.49	Trials to Oxted and Crowborough. Load 150 tons.
*	29.10.49	Light to Crowborough and Tunbridge Wells
	30.10.49	Light to Crowborough and Tunbridge Wells
	31.10.49	Trial to Crowborough. Load 161 tons.
*	1.11.49	Trials to Oxted and Crowborough. Load 153–255 tons.
	2.11.49	Trials to Oxted and Crowborough. Load 153–255 tons.
	3.11.49	Trials to Oxted and Crowborough. Load 153–255 tons.
	4.11.49	Trials to Oxted and Crowborough. Load 153–255 tons.
	7.11.49	Trials to Oxted, Polegate and Crowborough. Load 153–255 tons.
	8.11.49	Trials to Oxted, Polegate and Crowborough. Load 153–255 tons.
	9.11.49	Trials to Oxted, Polegate and Crowborough. Load 153–255 tons.
	10.11.49	Trials to Oxted, Polegate and Crowborough. Load 153–255 tons.
	11.11.49	Trials to Oxted, Polegate and Crowborough. Load 153–255 tons.
*	16.11.49	Trial to Oxted. Load 255 tons
	21.11.49	Trials to Oxted and Polegate. Load 153–255 tons.
	22.11.49	Trials to Oxted and Polegate. Load 153–255 tons.
	23.11.49	Trials to Oxted and Polegate. Load 153–255 tons.
	24.11.49	Trials to Oxted and Polegate. Load 153–255 tons.
*	25.11.49	Trials to Oxted and Polegate. Load 153–255 tons.
*	29.11.49	Trial to Polegate. Load 153 tons.
	1.12.49	Trials to Polegate, Oxted, Tunbridge Wells and Groombridge. Load 153–255 tons.
	2.12.49	Trials to Polegate, Oxted, Tunbridge Wells and Groombridge. Load 153–255 tons.
	3.12.49	Trials to Polegate, Oxted, Tunbridge Wells and Groombridge. Load 153–255 tons.
	4.12.49	Trials to Polegate, Oxted, Tunbridge Wells and Groombridge. Load 153–255 tons.
	5.12.49	Trials to Polegate, Oxted, Tunbridge Wells and Groombridge. Load 153–255 tons.
*	6.12.49	Trials to Polegate, Oxted, Tunbridge Wells and Groombridge. Load 153–255 tons.
	12.12.49	Trials to Crowborough and Oxted. Load 153–255 tons
*	13.12.49	Trials to Crowborough and Oxted. Load 153–255 tons.
	16.12.49	Light to Eastleigh and return.
	27. 1.50	Light to Tunbridge Wells.
	2. 2.50	Light to Eastleigh and return

* Signifies runs classed as failures.

A JUSTIFICATION TO SURVIVE

Part Two – The tests from Eastleigh

'Leader' was moved from Brighton on 13.4.50 and spent four days in store at Eastleigh before entering the works under whose auspices it would now remain. Prior to the dynamometer car tests the works were to continue to try to overcome the problem of the unbalanced weight distribution and, it was decided to add balancing weights within the corridor space at floor level. These took the form of several transverse struts filled with old brake blocks, firebars and other items of pig iron to a cumulative depth of almost 2ft. Even such drastic measures were insufficient and recourse had to be made to pieces of slab steel, both underneath the floor and vertically along the inside of the casing. An extra 5¼ tons was added in this way.

At the same time additional distance pieces were tried under the spring spigots. The final result was a far more acceptably balanced engine but one which now possesed a

No. 36001 inside Eastleigh running shed and probably soon after transfer from Brighton. It is reported that at no time was a boiler washout ever carried out on the engine. The T.I.A. water treatment was sufficient to prevent the accumulation of scale. This treatment involved the use of the manual blow down cock, with the discharge via the outlet near the throatplate, this was recalled as a very noisy operation. It is also reported that tube cleaning was rarely, if ever performed.

Collection of Les Warnett

Just passing Eastleigh South en-route for Fratton. No. 36001 is at the head of what appears to be a five-coach train.

S.C. Townroe

maximum axle loading of 24½ tons, 25% greater than that originally intended. With work hampered by pressure from more mundane matters it was not until the end of May that the engine was once again ready for service.

Because of all this extra weight, fresh authority had to be obtained from the Chief Civil Engineer for the engine to run at all. A decision was made allowing trials to be be undertaken only on routes cleared for the Merchant Navy class. The 50 mph speed limit imposed during the latter part of 1949 was also confirmed as were the restrictions in the amount of coal and water that could be carried. All this was intended to reduce the risk of damage to trackwork and bridges.

By 5.6.50, final adjustments of the ballast weights were complete and the engine was deemed ready for the next series of trials. It had been notified by now that it was the Eastern Region dynamometer car that would be used for the comparative tests, this particular vehicle having recorded the highest ever speed for a steam engine when run behind the world record holder *Mallard* in 1938. This time though high speed was not what was required, instead it was a justification for the future survival of No. 36001 and her sisters. Indeed, much would depend upon the data received.

Preliminary trials commenced on 6.6.50, with 'Leader' taking a rake of 10 coaches weighing some 332 tons over the 18 or so miles from Eastleigh to Fratton and return. The engine was initially handled by the works trials crew, although a number of other observers were also on board.

Short as it was, the run was not without its amusing incident. For as one of the works fitters recalled, ' . . . . when running well near Botley there was a lurch caused by the track, immediately following which a signal post came within a whisper of being wiped out . . . . we all held our breath.' The intention of the preliminary trials was to show up any minor modifications needed before the full dress runs and early results were

At Eastleigh again and on another of the preliminary trials to Fratton. The lighter coloured panel towards the centre of the engine was where the BR emblem had once been affixed. Why this was removed is unclear, was someone embarrased perhaps by the venture even at the start?

Collection of Mrs Talbot

Awaiting departure from Fratton for what was probably Eastleigh even if the headcode refers to the coast line to Brighton. The available line capacity on the Botley and Fareham line was the reason this was chosen for the early tests.

D.R. Yarney

promising. The return working for example was brought to a standstill near Eastleigh South Signalbox and then pulled away without a trace of hesitation or slip and still with a trailing load of 332 tons.

Following two more days on which similar tests were made, 'Leader' was stopped on 9.6.50 for attention to the grate and main steam pipes. Around the same time a partition type screen was installed to the rear of the driving position at No. 1 end and intended to reduce the heat radiating forward into the cab from the smokebox door. Unfortunately its presence made the task of smokebox cleaning even more difficult.

Notification had been received at Eastleigh that the dynamometer car would arrive towards the end of June, and the test staff anticipated undertaking two weeks of trials with 'Leader' during the first half of July following which comparative runs with a Southern 'Mogul' would be made. The route selected was from Eastleigh to Woking and return, allowing for suitable assessment of steaming capabilites over the gradients involved.

However, before these runs could begin the matter of crews had to be resolved, for the reputation of 'Leader' as an unpleasant machine on which to work had reached the ears of the locomen at the nearby running shed who would now be responsible for the test runs. The representative of the loco men on the L.D.C. committee stated that in principle they should have been consulted about the working conditions on 'Leader' and as this had not been the case they felt unable to assist with the tests. The way out of this impasse was for a volunteer crew to work the engine for trial purposes only. So Mr. Townroe as Shed Master posted a notice asking if there were any offers. Two men in the relief gang came forward, Driver Alf Smith and Fireman Sam Talbot, although they did so only on the condition that the runs were made with the slightly cooler No. 2, or bunker end leading. This pair were responsible for all the runs subsequently made from Eastleigh. Indeed if either was not available the engine did not leave the shed. Later both were to receive considerable accolades within the official reports of the runs for they contributed much under what were at times the most extraneous circumstances.

'Leader' and car outside Eastleigh shed. Despite Sam Talbot being the only Eastleigh shed fireman to work the engine on trial, a number of other firemen were detailed to assist in preparation and disposal duties. Few of these men had anything particularly complimentary to say about it.

D. Callender

To test the repairs to the grate and steam pipes a train of 10 coaches totalling 337 tons was taken to Woking on 12.6.50. Even before starting this trial there was a new difficulty and this time no fault of 'Leader'. For in 1950 the Bournemouth line was congested almost to capacity and it was a very difficult proposition to find a suitable spare path in which to run the trials. Consequently the only place available was immediately behind the 5.05 p.m. Bournemouth West to Waterloo passenger train, which on the day in question was in the charge of *Lord Nelson* No. 30852. Therefore, following the Waterloo train clearing the section ahead, Leader pulled smartly out onto the main line and on passing Shawford was said to be going as well as No. 30852; indeed those on board were fearful of a signal check as they were likely to catch up! But such success was short lived for less than one mile further on at Shawford Junction steam pressure began to fall, first to 240 p.s.i. and then to 190 p.s.i. and of course the route was still uphill all the way to Litchfield summit, 17 miles from Eastleigh. Consequently it was necessary for a stop to be made at Micheldever for a 'blow-up'.

After the boiler had rallied sufficiently, the trial continued despite being in official terms deemed a failure because of the enforced stop. At Woking there was a short turnaround after which a long delay occurred waiting for a path for the return run. Arrival back at Eastleigh was not until 2.30 a.m. next morning. The engine worked bunker end first on the up journey and smokebox first on the return.

Investigation at Eastleigh soon located the cause of the poor steaming, a buckled flange plate which meant the smokebox door was drawing air. Accordingly the necessary repairs were effected.

Trials resumed on 15.6.50 but this time with the slightly reduced load of 320 tons. Again steaming difficulties and the need for a 'breather' en-route caused the run to be classified as a failure.

Smith and Talbot had by now a chance to assess the engine for themselves, finding

Head on at No. 1 end and ready to begin the dynamometer car trials. The hole cut into the end was to facilitate connecting the various cables between the engine and test vehicle. This opening had been provided during one of the engines visits to Eastleigh Works when a welder suddenly appeared and proceeded to burn away the metal. 'What are you doing that for . . . ?' asked a bemused worker nearby, 'B------d if I know, I'm just doing what I was told', replied the welder, and picking up his tools he walked away.

Les Elsey

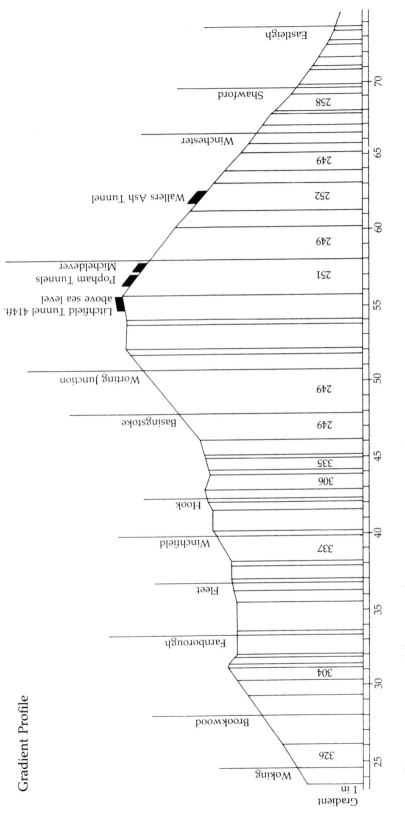

Gradient Profile

Eastleigh

Shawford 258

Winchester 249

Wallers Ash Tunnel 252

249

Micheldever 251
Popham Tunnels

Litchfield Tunnel 414ft. above sea level

Worting Junction 249

Basingstoke 249

335
306

Hook

Winchfield 337

Fleet

Farnborough

304

Brookwood

326

Woking

Gradient 1 in

Distances measured from London

The broken crank axle from 'Leader' in Eastleigh works shortly after it was removed from the bogie. A number of reasons were suggested for this failure, including the unsymmetrical drive, lack of movement in the horns, faulty manufacture or even poor design

J. Bell

some of the rumours true and others not so. What was certain was the associated heat and condensation. Much of the former was caused by the injectors beneath the cab of the centre compartment, and the mass of internal pipework within the casing was a continual source of dripping water.

It had been intended for the trips to continue on 19.6.50 but the trial was cancelled and instead the engine entered the works the next day for checking the valve events. At the same time the blast pipe cap was changed and the welding of the boiler examined. What had prompted the examination of the boiler is not recorded. A start was also made towards the fitting of the various items of test equipment needed for the dynamometer car trials.

Because of the sleeve valve design, checking the valve events on 'Leader' was a difficult and time consuming task. As a 'one-off' there was no suitable jig available and so it was necessary to move the engine along an inch at a time with pinch bars. This last task was made slightly easier because of the roller bearings fitted to all the axles and consequently one man could shift the 130+ ton engine by hand with consummate ease.

The dynamometer car, (No. 902532) arrived at Eastleigh on 29.6.50, coinciding with 'Leader' being booked for a further preliminary trial to Woking on eight coaches. This time the trouble began at the start, for on leaving Eastleigh a knocking noise was heard, different from anything else so far experienced and which appeared to be emanating from somewhere on No.1 bogie. Nevertheless for the moment the test continued. But nine miles from the start near Winchester Junction, the noise changed to a deep hammer sound, and appeared to be corresponding with each revolution of the wheels. The

The dynamometer car from the rear. Despite its antiquated appearance this vehicle contained much sophisticated recording equipment and had also been used in the locomotive exchange trials two years previously. It now resides in the National Railway Museum at York.

D. Callender

decision was made to halt the trial at Micheldever and 'Leader' was worked back to Eastleigh as gently as possible.

After the fire had been dropped at the running shed the engine was towed around to the works. Ostensibly this visit was pre-planned as some connections still had to be made with the dynamometer car, but of course the hammer noise had to be investigated. At first it was thought that the right hand valve and cylinder may have fractured but this was soon ruled out and instead attention was concentrated on the centre crank axle. But before this could be examined the body would have to be completely removed and so Brighton were asked to forward the two wooden trestles specially made to support the superstructure. These arrived on 3.7.50, together with an assortment of spares where-upon the bogies were fully removed and the fault at last revealed. The centre crank axle of No. 1 bogie had sheared at one end where the axle joined the wheel.

Not unnaturally there was an immediate call for a check to be made on the same component on No. 2 bogie to see if there were any signs of a similar fault. Tests were also carried out on both crank axles with mechanical and X-ray techniques. Similar results were found on each axle, pointing the conclusions towards a possible design fault rather than any metalurgical defect.

The whole future programme was now in doubt again, for how could the Railway Executive sanction the continuance of trials in the light of the latest findings? Surprisingly Riddles was adamant that the runs must continue as arranged and so instructions were issued for the engine to be fitted with two replacement crank axles and repaired where necessary in order that it might continue running. The replacement parts were taken from those intended for either Nos. 36004 or 36005.

With No. 36001 under repair yet again it was agreed the best course of action was to run the comparative trials with the 'Mogul', a 'U' class 2-6-0, No. 31618 was selected.

Sam Talbot was the fireman on 'Leader' during nearly all the trial runs from Eastleigh. He is shown here some years after the tests in the cab of a Crompton diesel.

Collection of Mrs Talbot

The dynamometer car runs using No. 31618 started on 10.7.50 and ironically only reached Basingstoke, for in the words of the test crew the engine was. '. . . in a poor condition and had amongst its defects a hot left hand trailing axlebox'. Accordingly the run was terminated and No. 31618 returned to Eastleigh for repair.

A different engine of the same class was now chosen, No. 31630 which was successfully modified with test fittings so as to be ready to commence trials by the end of July. No. 31630 was a totally different machine to her sister and performed well from the start. Three return trips between Eastleigh and Woking were completed on consecutive days, the last on 2.8.50. Each run was carried out with due observance to the set 50 mph test limit stipulated for 'Leader' and so the timings were set for an average speed of 40–45 mph. Throughout these and the subsequent runs the test staff were those from the Eastern Region who were given a free hand to conduct the trials in the way their experience dictated. In all cases the coal used was 'South Kirby Hards No. 1' and weighed into 1 cwt bags.

Meanwhile back at Eastleigh repairs progressed steadily on No. 36001, although as some in authority regarded 'Leader' as little more than an unmitigated nuisance there was perhaps not the urgency to the task. Finally by 14.8.50 work was at last completed and steam raised for a light engine trial to Botley the following day. This was again under the charge of the works trials crew. The trip was repeated the following day, a note in the records referring to the fact that some 2,000 gallons of water were used in each direction – a distance of less than five miles.

Another test had been planned for 17.8.50 but it was cancelled as a connecting rod from No. 2 bogie was striking the oil bath. Only minor repairs were needed this time and after a further light engine trial to Fratton on Friday 18.8.50, 'Leader' was moved to the running shed in preparation of the dynamometer car trials to commence after the weekend.

On No. 1 road at Eastleigh during the weekend of 19/20 August 1950 and when final adjustments were being made in preparation for the trials.

D.W. Winkworth

So on Monday 21.8.50 the long awaited trials at last began, No. 36001 steaming away from Eastleigh on a fine summer evening and with eight coaches in tow weighing some 231½ tons. All the trials were again scheduled as evening runs for the reason of line occupancy. In addition to the official observers, a fitter was booked on at the same time as Messrs. Smith & Talbot. The fitter would then assist with any preparations necessary although from the drivers point of view very little needed to be attended to as the use of oil baths and pressure lubrication meant there were only two oiling points on the whole engine.

The official report on the journey reads as follows;

'The start from Eastleigh was slow, and the boiler pressure fell quickly from 270 to 210lbs in six minutes, although the regulator was only partially open with 170lbs in the steam inlet pipes. Exhaust pressures of 12 and 12½lbs, and exhaust temperatures of 244 and 246 deg. Farenheit were noted, also a high smokebox vacuum of 5½ inches was recorded. Two minutes later, although the steam chest pressure had fallen to 140lbs. p.s.i. the exhaust temperatures continued to rise to 256 and 280 deg F. and the smokebox vacuum to 7 in. of water. The regulator was eased to give 100 p.s.i. in the steam chest and allow the steam pressure to rise in the boiler. The drawbar arm in ,the dynamometer car indicated unusual vibrations and as the exhaust temperatures continued to rise it was soon evident that all was not well with the engine working. Due to very hard work by the fireman the boiler pressure rose and was maintained at about 240 p.s.i. for the remainder of the journey. Under these conditions the temperature in the firemans cab was abnormal.' – the consequences of the high temperatures are explained in the report of the next run.

Leaving the north yard at Eastleigh and about to join the main line at Allbrook. No. 36001 makes a spirited get away on 21.8.50. Later analysis of the dynamometer car records would show 'Leader' used more oil for lubrication of the motion than a modern diesel used for fuel!

Les Elsey

Upon arrival at Woking the test ended at the south end of the Up yard. The engine and dynamometer car were then detached and the car propelled along the Portsmouth line to Guildford. Both units were then turned individually on the shed turntable and reconnected in anticipation of the return working.

At Guildford Smith and Talbot were able to enjoy a break while the engine was examined. Unfortunately this examination showed the mechanical lubricators of No. 2 bogie to be faulty and so to prevent the likelihood of seizure the test was abandoned with engine and car returning to Eastleigh light the next day.

Following repairs at the works another run was made on 23.8.50 this time with the increased load of 264½ tons.

'Prior to starting the up journey from Eastleigh . . . .steam was blowing from the safety valves, but the boiler pressure fell to 185 p.s.i. after 16 minutes. The exhaust pressures were again high and the exhaust temperatures gradually rose to 350 deg. F. which is the limit of the working range of temperature for the indicator in the dynamometer car for this purpose. In order to reduce the coal and water consumption the engine was worked in 20% cut off instead of 30% used on the previous test runs. Although this had the effect of reducing the smokebox vacuum the engine continued to throw burning char from the chimney top. The actual running time was spoilt by a number of signal checks, seven in all, and four signal stops, they assisted in keeping up the boiler pressure. On the return journey from Woking, steam was again blowing from the safety valves and a thicker fire was put on the grate before starting away. The regulator was adjusted to give a maximum steam chest

Shawford, 7.20 p.m., 24.8.50. The headcode signified a main line duty but the legend 'SPL' on the disc indicated a special working. Of all the photographs taken of the engine, both under construction and on test, there are few north of Eastleigh and none at all so far found north of this point.

R. Curl

pressure and the engine tried out in 15% cut off on the easier sections of the route. This resulted in maintaining a higher boiler pressure and reduced the exhaust steam temperatures within the range of measurement, but there was no improvement in either the coal or water consumption. The engine refused to start on one or two occasions and had to reverse before a drawbar pull of about 5 tons necessary to start the train could be exerted. All the figures and evidence collected at this stage was ample proof that a considerable amount of the steam produced was being wasted, either by leakage past the piston, or sleeve valves of both engine units.'

The last comment was borne out in another way. At Eastleigh the running staff had already experienced difficulties with excessive steam consumption and found an unofficial way to assist matters when the engine was cold. This was simply to run light engine up and down a short length of track a few times which then allowed the cylinders to warm through and hopefully expand the sleeves. Not surprisingly such behaviour was officially frowned upon.

The comments made with regard to the difficulty in starting are most interesting, for they follow almost exactly the problems encountered earlier with No. 2039. On 'Leader' any reluctance to start was overcome by means of the fitter dismounting and then pushing over the reverser with a crow-bar!

Back at Eastleigh in the early hours of 24.8.50, engine and car were again turned and stabled ready for another test later that day. This was to be with 10 coaches equal to 290½ tons.

> 'A fourth test run was made on 24.8.50. When running between Eastleigh motive power depot to the reception sidings to pick up the trainload the cylinder cocks were open to get rid of the condensation. The cylinder of No. 1 end can be seen from the dynamometer car and it was observed that an abnormal quantity of water was issuing from the sleeve valves. The condensed steam was white and oily from the lubrication supply. When attached to the train, the boiler pressure was 275 p.s.i., and again a good thickness of fire was on the firegrate. The weight of the train for this test run was 290½ tons, a light load for an engine of this size. Working in 30% cut off with 140 p.s.i. in the steam chest the boiler pressure fell rapidly to 200lbs. Good work by the fireman got the pressure back to 225lbs but the pressure fell to 140lbs approaching Winchester City, 7½ miles from the starting point, and a running time of 19 minutes. A stop had to be made to regain the boiler pressure but as this so upset the booked path, the test run was abandoned at Micheldever. On arrival back at Eastleigh depot a standing test very clearly showed that steam was blowing to waste and further tests with the engine in this condition was useless.'

Apparently while waiting at Micheldever for the return, an amount of water was taken by means of a ½in. hose connected to a standpipe on the cattle dock – reminiscences of the first run from Brighton.

Back at Eastleigh a decision had once again to be taken on the immediate future and accordingly Riddles was informed of this latest difficulty. The reply though was rapid, ' . . . . the tests must continue . . .', and so again contrary to what had been expected No. 36001 re-entered the works on 28.8.50 with attention focused on valves and pistons.

Three weeks were spent out of service on what involved considerable repairs. On No. 1 bogie a new sleeve was fitted to the left hand cylinder and a number of score marks on the other cylinders smoothed over. Similar repairs were affected to No. 2 bogie, with all the parts again obtained from Brighton and the incomplete engines of the class. In addition, all 144 rings surrounding the sleeves and pistons were renewed (20 on each sleeve and 4 per cylinder) with lesser work also carried out in other areas.

With the engine out of service the testing staff prepared an interim report on the runs so far. (This provides the quotes used in the chapter thus far.)

The engine was eventually released from the works on 20.9.50 and steamed for a light engine trip to Fratton the next day. This was in the charge of Smith and Talbot. The results were very promising and performance reported as '. . . better than at any time in the past.' Upon the return to Eastleigh arrangements were immediately put in hand for the conclusion of the tests, a final check on 22.9.50 revealed for the first time that no defects of any type required attention!

Accordingly on the evening of 25.9.50, No. 36001 left Eastleigh with eight coaches weighing 241½ tons. This was of course less than had been taken in the past, but the intention was to allow the sleeves and rings time to 'bed-in' before attempting a heavier train.

> 'EASTLEIGH – WOKING; The engine was worked mainly in 30% cut off and partial regulator to give 110 to 120lbs in the steam chest. As a result, the train speed rose gradually to 46 m.p.h. on the rising gradients to Litchfield Signal

'U' class 2-6-0 No. 1618 at Salisbury SR shed 20.9.47. Less than two years later as No. 31618 this engine was used in the comparative tests against 'Leader'. For the trials both No. 31618 and her replacement No. 31630 were run with a thin fire and care was taken to avoid undue waste of steam at both the safety valves and injectors. The choice of No. 31618 for comparative trials was itself interesting as she was always regarded as a poor performer and it was hoped the control runs would show up where the deficiencies were.

H.C. Casserley

Box. . . . .On the falling gradients from Basingstoke to Woking, the booked time was maintained, the maximum speed being 55½ m.p.h.'

'WOKING – EASTLEIGH; The engine was worked in 25% cut off with higher steam chest pressures. Signal checks spoilt the running to Brookwood, but with clear signals the steam chest pressure was put up to 200lbs and this gave a drawbar pull of 3.38 tons which accelerated the train from 20 to 41 m.p.h. in 1½ miles. The regulator was eased and at the 31½ mile post, the speed was 50.2 m.p.h. The maximum speed was 54 m.p.h. at mile post 44.'

The following day an extra vehicle was added, making nine in total and equal to 275 tons. As at Brighton any available vehicles were used. For Sam Talbot these runs were far more strenuous than a normal firing turn, his task hampered by the curved coal chute which tended to be anything but self feeding. Fortunately there was always an observer present to assist in moving the weighed bags of coal from the bunker. Even so only one fireman was ever carried per trip, while the number of observers together with the various lumps of scrap placed in the corridor as balance weights made the internal conditions rather cramped. From the fireman's viewpoint it was also difficult for him to gauge exactly where the train was at any time, especially as sound was distorted by the external casing of the engine.

26.9.50. 'EASTLEIGH – WOKING; Working mainly in 25% cut off to Shawford Junction, the speed rose to 42 m.p.h. and the exhaust pressure was

91

up to 14lbs with the result that a good amount of burning char was thrown from the chimney. The gear was changed to 20% cut off, but the exhaust pressure again rose to 14lbs when the speed was 53 m.p.h. When passing through Wallers Ash Tunnel at 53 m.p.h. there was a shower of large pieces of burning char from the chimney top. Sectional running time was maintained to Basingstoke. During the downhill running to Woking, a maximum speed of 56 m.p.h. was noted near Farnborough; this speed could have been exceeded if it had been desirable.

WOKING – EASTLEIGH; The engine put up a good performance by passing Brookwood at 42.5 m.p.h. a drawbar pull of 2.4 tons was maintained and the train speed rose to 50 m.p.h. at mile post 31.

27.9.50. Nine vehicles, equal to 294½ tons.
EASTLEIGH – WOKING; The load was again increased to test the engine when working with higher steam chest pressures. There was some difficulty in obtaining suitable conditions owing to steam blows from the cylinder release valves when the pressure in the cylinders was above 210 p.s.i. At 21 m.p.h., with a steam chest pressure of 195lbs, the drawbar pull was 3.48 tons, drawbar horsepower 872 and the exhaust pressure 15lbs. The boiler pressure gradually fell to 200lbs. The regulator was eased to 130lbs in the steam chest and the boiler pressure rose to 225lbs in three minutes. At this point speed was 51 m.p.h . . .
WOKING – EASTLEIGH: A relatively good performance was made on the continuously rising gradient of 1 in 389 during which the speed rose to 50 m.p.h. in 12 minutes . . . .'

The final trip with the dynamometer car was made on 28.9.50, this time with ten coaches of 325½ tons. From the remarks of the testing staff it was as if some of the steaming difficulties had at last been overcome, although there was still an amount of steam wastage referred to in the blow from the cylinder release valves. Smith and Talbot were also almost used to 'Leader' by now even if they voiced differing views. Alf Smith as driver liked the fact that he could perform his task seated although he was not happy to be separated from his fireman. Sam Talbot however voiced criticism of the working conditions as well as reiterating Smith's earlier comments. The comments made by the crew about being parted from each other should not be read lightly, for they were genuinely concerned as to each others welfare. Had for example 'Leader' ever been involved in an accident and overturned the fireman could well have been trapped. Certainly on all the tests there were always more than just the crew carried.

28.9.50. EASTLEIGH – WOKING; After passing onto the main line at Allbrook, the gear was set at 25% cut off. The speed rose to 50 m.p.h. in 12 minutes and the exhaust pressure rose to 12lbs with a pressure of 195lbs in the steam chest.

WOKING – EASTLEIGH. Special attention is drawn to the particulars of the engine performance from Woking when a speed of 50 m.p.h. was attained in 12 minutes 44 seconds. There was no difficulty in maintaining adequate boiler pressure. During this period 9 cwts of coal were put into the firebox. . . . .'

No doubt because this was the last trial, the engine was allowed more leeway on the return trip. The descent from Litchfield Summit to Eastleigh was taken at far more than the stipulated speed. (Unfortunately we do not know how much more!) Everything performed faultlessly with 'Leader' behaving in the way she had been intended. Back at Eastleigh the dynamometer car and train were uncoupled and the engine taken to the shed. After the fire had been dropped a chain was fastened around the access doors to prevent unauthorised entry. It seemed as if all now depended upon a decision by the Railway Executive.

Engine	No.36001 SR 'Leader' Class (Second Series)							
Train and Route	UP – 6.45 p.m. DOWN – 11.35 p.m.		Eastleigh–Woking Woking–Eastleigh				Special Empty Train	
	UP	DOWN	UP	DOWN	UP	DOWN	UP	DOWN
Date	25.9.50	25.9.50	26.9.50	26.9.50	27.9.50	27.9.50	28.9.50	28.9.50
No. Signal and P. Way Checks	2	6	1	3	4	0	1	0
No. Unbooked stops	1	4	0	2	4	1	1	3
Weight of Engine (in working order) (tons)	130.45	–	–	–	–	–	–	–
Weight of Train behind Drawbar (tons)	241.5	241.5	275.5	275.5	294.5	294.5	325.5	325.5
Train miles (actual)	48.87	49.05	48.825	49.03	48.98	49.03	48.97	49.07
Ton miles (excluding weight of engine)	11800	11840	13450	13500	144200	14440	15940	15970
Ton miles (including weight of engine)	18160	18240	19820	19900	20800	20820	22320	22360
Time booked running min	72	71	72	71	72	71	72	71
Time actual running min	78.45	94.48	71.67	82.15	87.47	74.03	72.98	82.90
Speed mph average	37.35	31.0	40.9	35.8	33.6	39.7	40.25	35.5
Work done h.p. hr	345.8	315.8	402.3	342.2	408.7	324.0	404.33	379.0
Average D.B. pull tons	1.185	1.078	1.380	1.169	1.398	1.105	1.385	1.294
Average D.B. h.p.	264.2	200.5	337.0	250.0	280.5	262.5	332.5	274.5
Coal Total weight lbs	2352	2464	2688	2464	2632	2240	2576	2240
Coal lbs/mile	48.20	50.25	55.00	50.30	53.80	45.70	52.60	45.65
Coal lbs/ton mile (excluding engine)	0.1995	0.2081	0.1997	0.1825	0.1825	0.1551	0.1616	0.1402
coal lbs/ton mile (including engine)	0.1296	0.1351	0.1356	0.1238	0.1266	0.1075	0.1154	0.1002
Coal lbs/hr (running time)	1800	1564	2250	1800	1806	1815	2118	1622
Coal lbs/sq. ft. Grate/hr (running time)	70.6	61.4	88.2	70.6	70.8	71.2	83.0	63.6
Coal lbs/D.B.h.p. hr	6.81	7.81	6.68	7.20	6.44	6.92	6.37	5.91
Water total gall	1807	1712	1927	1807	2000	1635	1987	1929
Water gall/mile	37.0	34.90	39.48	36.88	40.89	33.35	40.60	39.31
Water lbs/ton mile (including engine)	0.996	0.939	0.972	0.908	0.961	0.785	0.890	0.863
Water lbs/hr (running time)	13,820	10,860	16,130	13,200	13,720	13,250	16,340	13,960
Water lbs/sq. ft. heating surface/hr	5.79	4.55	6.76	5.53	5.75	5.55	6.85	5.85
Water lbs/D.B.h.p. hr	52.25	54.25	47.90	52.80	48.95	50.42	49.15	50.9
Evaporation actual lbs water/lb coal	7.68	6.95	7.18	7.33	7.60	7.30	8.61	
Evaporation from and at 212°F	10.17	9.10	9.50	9.54	9.92	9.60	10.16	11.30
Boiler efficiency %	71.9	66.0	67.2	69.1	70.4	71.1	72.0	83.7
Gross calorific value of coal B.Th. U/lb	13,660	13,315	13,660	13,315	13,640	13,055	13,635	13,055
B. Th.Us./D.B.H.P. hr	93025	103,990	91,248	95,868	87,906	90,341	86,855	77,155
Overall efficiency %	2.74	2.45	2.79	2.66	2.90	2.82	2.93	3.3
Weather conditions	Showery		Fine Dry Rail		Showery		Fine Dry Rail	

SUMMARY OF WEIGHINGS   No. 36001   PERIOD NOVEMBER 1949 – FEBRUARY 1950

Column groups: columns 1–4 under **No. 1. (Chimney) Bogie No.1**; columns 5–6 under **No. 2. End. (Water tank) Bogie No.2**; **Totals** = Bogie No.1 (T.c.), Bogie No.2 (T.c.), Grand (T.c.); **Increase of weight on right-side** = Bogie No.1 (T.c), Bogie No.2; then **Total**. Axle columns are in T. cwt.

Date	Water	Coal	No. of weighings		1	2	3	4	5	6	Bogie No.1	Bogie No.2	Grand	Incr. Bogie No.1	Incr. Bogie No.2	Total
5.11.49 Brighton	4000 galls	Approx 4 tons	1	Right	10 19	13 0	13 14	13 16	15 5	9 9	37 13	38 10	76 7	12 2	8 15	20 17
				Left	11 0	7 4	7 15	6 10	10 6	12 19	25 15	29 15	55 10			
				Total	21 19	20 4	21 9	20 6	25 11	22 8	63 12	68 5	131 17			
16.12.49 Eastleigh	4000 galls + a glass	4 tons	Average of 3	Right	10 19	12 2	10 8	11 14	13 4	11 10	33 9	36 8	69 17	4 15	4 9	9 4
				Left	7 2	10 4	11 8	7 10	11 9	13 0	28 14	31 19	60 13			
				Total	18 1	22 6	21 16	19 4	24 13	24 10	62 3	68 7	130 10			
16.12.49 Eastleigh	200 + galls + ¾ a glass	3 tons	Average of 3	Right	10 10	10 1	10 12	10 11	11 18	8 15	31 3	31 4	62 7	1 5	3 4	4 9
				Left	8 14	10 17	10 7	6 15	8 16	12 9	29 18	28 0	57 18			
				Total	19 4	20 18	20 19	17 6	20 14	21 4	61 1	59 4	120 5			
16.12.49 Eastleigh	Tanks empty glass	Bunker empty	Average of 2	Right	9 18½	11 0½	9 18½	7 14½	8 18½	8 17½	30 17½	25 10½	56 8	1 11	0 8	1 19
				Left	9 4½	8 13½	11 8½	6 7	7 13½	11 2	29 6½	25 2½	54 9			
				Total	19 3	19 14	21 7	14 1½	16 12	19 19½	60 4	50 13	110 17			
2.2.50 Eastleigh	Tanks empty glass	Bunker empty	Average of 3	Right	12 2	9 14	9 15	10 9	9 16	9 1	31 11	29 6	60 17	3 15	5 9	9 4
				Left	7 8	10 8	10 0	7 3	9 13	7 1	27 16	23 17	51 13			
				Total	19 10	20 2	19 15	17 12	19 9	16 2	59 7	53 3	112 10			
2.2.50 Eastleigh	3000 galls + a glass	3 tons	Average of 3	Right	12 7	10 11	10 12	13 0	11 5	11 8	33 10	35 13	69 3	5 18	4 16	10 14
				Left	8 4	10 7	9 1	8 15	11 10	10 12	27 12	30 17	58 9			
				Total	20 11	20 18	19 13	21 15	22 15	22 0	61 2	66 10	127 12			

The Eastleigh weigh-table was capable of registering maximum axle load of up to 25 tons per axle. Apparently when first weighed and before the modifications to the pedestals, the pointers had been forced right off the end of the calibrations. One observer recounting that in his opinion the true weight on one occasion was nearer 30 ton axle maximum. As stated though, this must be taken as an *unconfirmed* report.

COMPARATIVE TESTS WITH SOUTHERN REGION LOCOMOTIVES

Train 6.45 p.m. Eastleigh–Woking
Date: 25.9.50
Record No. 1840.

Particulars of temperatures, pressures, etc.
Engine No. 36001   Southern Region Class 'Leader'

| Time | Speed m.p.h. | DB Pull tons Actual | Pressure lbs/sq. in. | | | | | S'box Vacuum (in.) | Temperatures °F | | | | | | Reg'r position | Cut off (%) |
| | | | Steam Chest | | Exhaust | | Boiler | | Smokebox | | Inlet steam | | Exhaust | | | |
			No. 1	No.2	No.1	No.2	Boiler		A	B	No.1	No.2	No.1	No.2		
6.51	15	1.80	110	100	1	½	230	1½	530	560	435	415	220	220	¼	30
6.54	25	2.66	140	140	5½	5	230	4	580	630	500	490	230	232	¼	30
6.57	35	2.16	115	120	5	5	230	3¾	580	640	540	565	238	240	¼	30
7.01	39	1.81	120	115	7½	5	225	4¾	630	680	560	595	268	246	¼	30
7.03	42	2.04	–	115	–	6½	245	–	–	–	590	620	283	260	¼	30
7.05	45	1.79	110	105	7½	7	235	5	640	690	605	655	322	304	¼	30
7.11	45	1.80	110	110	8¼	8¼	230	5¼	630	690	600	665	348	328	¼	30
7.14	46	1.92	120	120	10	11½	265	5½	660	700	605	670	350*	335	¼	30
7.18	46	1.94	110	110	10	10	245	5½	640	690	605	670	350*	348	¼	30
7.20	52	.80	70	75	4	2¾	240	1	590	640	595	655	350*	350	⅛	15
7.24	20	1.50	–	115	–	¾	220	–	–	–	550	610	350	296	¼	15
7.50	32	2.26	135	140	5¾	4½	225	4	530	565	450	500	296	240	¼	20
7.53	55	1.11	–	80	–	4	250	–	–	–	500	560	310	262	⅛	20
8.00	52	.78	30	60	2½	1¾	240	1½	530	570	505	555	324	278	⅛	20
8.04	50	.80	50	55	3	1¼	250	1½	510	560	510	555	322	276	⅛	20
8.07	51	.98	55	65	4	2	240	2½	540	570	510	555	312	278	⅛	20
8.16	46	1.50	–	95	–	3¾	220	–	–	–	540	570	304	250	¼	20
Averages			98	101	5¾	4¾	236	3½	584	630	540	580	340	280		

No.1 Smokebox End   Positions   A. in front of large tubes   *Limit of range of instrument in Dynamometer Car.
                                        B. in front of small tubes.

AN OPPORTUNITY LOST ?

Following the conclusion of the official test runs No. 36001 stood cold and lifeless at the rear of Eastleigh shed awaiting a decision as to her future. To those of Bulleids' former staff who had been involved in the project from its inception it must have seemed as if the result was a foregone conclusion.

Within the Southern Region however there was a school of thought which felt the engine had not yet been given the opportunity to perform in the way in which the design had intended. Therefore, in early October 1950 arrangements were put in hand for what was to be the final series of trials. Before these could be undertaken the engine and boiler were again thoroughly checked and a number of necessary repairs made. These included the renewal of the flexible steam pipes to the generators as well as a number of flange joints connecting the blower and associated components.

As a prelude, a trial run was arranged from Eastleigh to Cosham on 14 October with Messrs. Smith and Talbot once more in charge. All was satisfactory and so the full test was set for three days later on 17 October.

So near and yet so far, No. 36002 in store at Brighton. The engine only required the external covers to the axlebox springs, steam and vacuum pipes and cab windows and she would have been ready for trials. It was said to be just two days work. What is not known is if the modifications carried out to No. 36001 were incorporated in the second engine as the work progressed. If not one could foresee the same problems all over again.

Collection of D. Broughton

96

No. 36003, No. 1 end, with No. 36002 behind in store at Bognor Regis steam shed, 1.7.50. Officially both engines were moved here because of a shortage of storage space at Brighton, but it may also have been an attempt to remove the project from the public gaze. Nos. 36002 and 36003 had also spent a period in store at New Cross, Gate Shed, London. Both were finally cut up at Brighton.

Collection of D. Broughton

On the day of the actual run No. 36001 was coupled up to 13 coaches weighing 430 tons and with the route the same as for the previous dynamometer car trials, viz Eastleigh to Basingstoke–Woking and Guildford returning the same way. Again Smith and Talbot crewed, with in addition a senior member of the Railway Executive on board, Roland Bond. One observer who witnessed the departure described the start as '. . . effortless . . .', a most interesting comment bearing in mind that this start was with in excess of a 100 tons greater trailing load compared with anything attempted on previous trials.

Unfortunately such good fortune was not destined to continue, for at the customary Basingstoke water stop the engine refused to move either forward or back and some six minutes were wasted attempting to draw up to the water column. Such eccentricies of behaviour were hardly likely to impress Mr Bond. The remainder of the run was without incident, the return working south of Basingstoke achieved at a speed much greater than anything so far obtained. It was almost as if 'Leader' herself was trying to make up for its earlier misdemeanour at Basingstoke.

The official record of the run however contained a certain amount of criticism;

> 'The engine ran satisfactorily and whilst some time was lost on the easier sections, this could well have been avoided by slightly heavier working. The steam pressure and water level were fairly well maintained, but steaming was not entirely satisfactory during the heaviest working conditions. The performance of the locomotive was such, however, as to indicate that a trial could be attempted with 480 tons.'

No. 36004 in embryo form and consisting just of main frames and boiler. The coach bogies were merely to allow the components to be moved around the yard area. Nos. 36004/5 had not reached anywhere near the stage of construction of the other engines, both little more than a collection of parts which were robbed to provide spares for No. 36001. Both Nos. 36004/5 were eventually taken away for disposal in goods waggons.

W.N.J. Jackson

Leader was being given one last chance to redeem herself and 2 November was the date set for what was to be the final test. Again the same crew were in charge on the same route.

Coupled to no less than 15 coaches, amounting to some 480 tons No. 36001 left Eastleigh in the early November gloom heading north. The only concession made was an extra 5 min. in the passing time to Winchester Junction and considered necessary because of the heavy load to be hauled unaided on the long climb from Eastleigh.

This time there was no senior observer, but such was the performance of the engine that 50 mph was maintained almost throughout, while at Micheldever the safety valves lifted indicating too much steam was available. Passing Worting the train was ½ minute early although a signal stop meant arrival at Basingstoke was a little delayed. An official account of the run to this point referred to the performance thus;

> 'The performance on this test was far in excess of anything previously attained, the estimated power output corrected for gradient, being of the order of 1100 h.p. at the drawbar. Steam temperatures were not taken due to the failure of the instrument.'

Certainly all on board must have looked forward to the remainder of the run. But it was not to be, for while taking water the opportunity was taken for a check around the engine where it was found that the smokebox door was slightly ajar. Had the demands for steam not previously been so prolific this would probably have mattered little, but as it was the power output obtained had caused an amount of cinders and char to fall out of the door and which now threatened to set the wooden lagging and floor alight, whilst

The incomplete No. 36003 at Brighton. A considerable amount of work was needed on this engine before it would have been ready for steam trials. She is shown being shunted by the Brighton works shunter at the latter location on 23.5.51 and just before final cutting up. Work on the 'Leader' class and specifically Nos. 36002/3 was responsible for the delay in completing Nos. 34091–94 a batch of 'Light Pacifics' at Brighton. The Pacifics not appearing in traffic until the Autumn of 1949 several months later than had originally been intended.

Collection of D. Broughton

the door itself was badly warped. There was then no alternative but to abandon the test and return to Eastleigh, No. 36001 leaving her train in the sidings at Basingstoke and heading south for Eastleigh light engine.

Even so it was not quite over, as speed was again worked up to a very high rate, some reports speak of as much as 90 mph and without a hint of trouble from any quarter, indeed the engine rode as smoothly as a coach. Upon arrival at Eastleigh it transpired that the failure was simply due to human error, a workman who had omitted to ensure the smokebox door was secure before the engine had left the shed. Even so all that was required was a replacement smokebox door and a number were available from the unfinished sisters to No. 36001. But it was not to be and with her fire dropped, No. 36001 was shunted to an empty siding alongside the shed, she would never steam again.

Bulleid himself was by now well ensconsed as Chief Mechanical Engineer to the C.I.E. in Eire and so could only receive reports on No. 36001 via members of his former Southern staff. As previously stated Riddles had also dictated that work on No. 36001's sister engines be suspended, Nos. 36002–5 were stored in various stages of completion. This fact too was communicated to Bulleid, which almost certainly led to a small delegation of officials from the Irish Railways visiting Brighton with a view to purchasing the incomplete machines.* However, nothing further come of the visit.

* Recorded in correspondance between the writer and the late Don Bradley author of several books on locomotives.

'Leader' on trial and awaiting departure from Brighton Station. The engine never worked any revenue earning trains and so the choice of commencing tests from the passenger station was to simulate realistic operating conditions. This was the photograph reproduced in the American journal, *Mechanical Engineering* with the caption. '. . . Leader class engine in service'. The alternating light and dark patches on the side sheeting is thought to be accentuated by side lighting.

National Railway Museum

CC1 the Irish Turf Burner, awaiting the cutters torch at Inchicore in 1963. The similarity with the original 'Leader' design is obvious and it was to fail for reasons of politics. Some lessons though had been learnt, for the boiler was placed centrally about the chassis and with a joint compartment for the driver and fireman. The 'engine' units too were improved and removable from the power bogies.

Colin Boocock

Was Bulleid then intent on producing a new 'Leader'? indeed he was, with the first hint of this in an article in the journal *Mechanical Engineering* (1950) under the title 'Locomotive and Rolling Stock Developments in Great Britain.'

The article set out to show how steam locomotive development had taken place, with obvious preference given to Bulleid's own achievements. A detailed description was given of 'Leader' and included several photographs. One of these showed the prototype about to depart from Brighton with a test train and the slightly misleading caption of 'Leader class engine in service.'

The text which was obviously written before the final runs with No. 36001 included;

> 'While in American eyes this is a small engine, its horsepower will be about 1700 and consequently it will give as good results as a Diesel-Electric locomotive with a 2000 h.p. engine. How successful we have been in the new design remains to be seen, but the new features in the engine should give us better service, help to improve the performance of the steam locomotive and restore steam traction to favour.'

A few sentences after there is a direct clue as to the future direction of Bulleid's work and which with hindsight may be taken to include the knowledge that No. 36001 was already doomed even before publication of the official BR report;

> 'While in this Leader class of engine the developments of the steam locomotive has been carried a stage further, there is still much work to be done. The use of the blast to create draft should give way to fans so that we can control the production of steam accurately. The exhaust steam should not be allowed to escape to the atmosphere but should be returned to the boiler. Experimental work already done encourages the thought that these two problems can be solved, and I commend them to the young engineers as worthy of investigation. I shall feel more than recompensed if I have shown that while the Stephenson locomotive may in some circumstances be dead or dying, this cannot be said of steam traction itself. If new designs be developed in the light of our present greater knowledge and the servicing of the locomotive be brought up to date – in short, if only we can demolish the conservatism which is destroying the steam locomotive rather than give up any of its customary ways – then we can look forward to a revival of steam traction.'

But what was Bulleid trying to say, was it a vindication of the existing 'Leader' design or a veiled hint towards another progression of steam or perhaps another new 'Leader'? In fact it was probably both, for he was already formulating the ideas which were to develop into the Irish turf burning engine and which was in effect Leader Mk. 2.*

In the meantime on the Southern Region the report of the dynamometer car tests, including the comparative runs against the 'U' class engine had been published. As was expected there was considerable criticism of the design which was hardly surprising after the number of problems that had occurred. (Extracts from the report are reproduced as Appendix D.)

But what the dynamometer car did not do was draw any positive conclusions and

---

* The Turf Burner is described briefly in Appendix I.

101

Forlorn and lifeless, No. 36001, the only 'Leader' to steam on trials awaiting the cutters torch at Eastleigh in 1951. Bulleid is reputed to have said that had the engine been intended for use on other railways then water pick-up gear and more coal would have been carried. Many years later Robin Riddles, the former BR Chief Mechanical Engineer when interviewed said about Bulleid, 'As a man I liked him and we got on well, but he was an individualist who wanted to do it his own way, and some of what he did was questionable. I couldn't fathom some of his thinking.' When asked about the decision to scrap 'Leader' he continued, 'It was the only sensible decision to make. The thing was 30 tons overweight, and the boiler so badly balanced it needed 2½ tons of pig-iron on one side to balance it up. Apart from that, the fireman was forced to stand so close to the firebox he was burning himself. The fireman had to lag himself with sandbags to deflect the heat. Was there a job for Bulleid after Nationalisation? – No, how could there be. Having been king of his own dungheap, how could he suddenly come and serve in mine? The surprise to me was that having failed on the Southern, he went to Ireland and failed there too.'

Lens of Sutton

instead this was left to R.A. Riddles in his memorandum to the Railway Executive dated 20 November 1950.

The report dealt with the progression of the tests to date as well as the various remedies attempted in an effort to overcome problems. – see Appendix H. Midway through came the first damning statement;

'There are only two alternatives which now present themselves in respect of the future of this class of locomotive. They are;

a) To make a number of major modifications to the present design with a view to overcoming the difficulties which have been experienced and the deficiencies which have been revealed.

or:–

b) To scrap the locomotive so far completed and the other four in varying stages of construction.'

1-Co-Co-1 Diesel Electric No. 10201 passing Basingstoke with the 1.0 p.m. Waterloo–Exeter express, 29.3.55. All three of these Southern diesels used the same body to bogie mounting as on 'Leader' which gave trouble-free service throughout their lives. Later still the BR class 40, 45 and 46 diesels would adopt a similar mounting. Bulleid was of course principally a steam man and although the body shell and underframe of the diesel were to his own design, the internal mechanisms were not. The body profile matches well with the design of his coaches behind. These engines were popular with their crews for they sported a hot plate, wash basin and lavatory for the crew, enabling both driver and fireman to go home clean from a shift.

P.J. Kelley

The various changes required in accordance with option (a) were then listed in detail – again see Appendix H, after which came the final judgement.

'Expenditure amounting to £178,865 has already been incurred. So far it has not been possible, nor will it be possible to place this locomotive in revenue earning service without further heavy expense. I have not estimated what this further expense might be because, even if it were incurred and all the defects eliminated the locomotive, as modified, would offer no advantages compared with one of conventional well-tried design.

I am compelled, therefore to RECOMMEND that the second alternative namely, the completed locomotive and the the four in various stages of construction, should be scrapped and that the authority for their construction as part of the 1948 Locomotive Building Programme should be cancelled.'

In just two brief paragraphs 'Leader' was effectively killed off. But the question remains was it the right decision to make? Faced with this evidence Riddles had no other choice at that time. The railways had insufficient funding to develop such a radical new steam design whilst it was already recognised in 1950 that steam as the prime mover was to be eliminated as soon as possible.

The centre pivotless bogie for diesel electric No. 10202 outside Ashford Works in June 1951. The body mounting pads can be discerned on either side of the centre driven axle.

Les Elsey

This may at first appear strange, especially as in 1950 all four regions were still building steam engines to pre-nationalisation designs and the final range of BR standard designs were still to emerge. However, with thought the reasons become clearer, what was needed was a range of conventional 'go anywhere, cope with anything' designs as indeed the 'Standards' would become. 'Leader' just did not fit in.

Back at Eastleigh No. 36001 still languished alongside the shed, its sister engines towed away from the public eye into store, first at New Cross, then Bognor Regis before returning to Brighton and the cutters torch. The pioneer No. 36001 remained in the open until the evening of 25 April 1951 when she was towed to the adjacent Eastleigh Works for cutting. A few weeks later most of the engine had been completely dismantled although parts from the bogies remained by the works oil store for several years.

It was hoped to utilise the roller bearings from the 'Leader' engines for the centre axles of the 'Q1' class, but in the event the amount of modification that would have been required meant such a consideration had to be abandoned.

Quietly BR no doubt believed the whole project could be quickly forgotten, but the railway press refused to be silenced as per a correspondent for the *Railway Gazette* on 25 May 1951 who asked;

> 'I wonder if an appeal could be made through your columns for more information about this design? I know of no official information or photographs published about this interesting class although it is now two years since the first one appeared from Brighton Works. (As can be seen within the text numerous official views WERE taken of 'Leader' and contemporary documentary evidence recorded. – KJR.) As far as my information goes only one 'Leader' class locomotive has ever been steamed and that has been lying out of use in the open at Eastleigh since early November. If this locomotive

The principles of 'Leader', a BR Mk. 6 bogie and with the same damping and cushioning arrangement as on 'Leader'.

Ian Shawyer

design is unfortunately unsuccessful there may be an attempt in official quarters to forget that it ever existed as has happened in the past with some experimental designs. It seems odd that the extensive trials with this locomotive should appear to have been abandoned just when they appeared to be meeting with a fair measure of success. The locomotive apparently made several quite successful runs to Woking about last October.'

The reply from BR was curt;

'. . . . for varying technical reasons the experiments with the prototype 'Leader' class locomotive were not as satisfactory as had been hoped and to obviate the expense which would be involved in continuing them for a problematical return, it has been decided not to proceed further with this novel design.'

As such BR decreed the matter was closed, any further attempt by outside individuals to glean more information was either politely refused or stone-walled against the harshness of officialdom.

Such an attitude no doubt contributed to the aura surrounding the engine which consistantly refused to subside. It finally culminated in the dramatic revelations of the *Sunday Dispatch* on 18 January, 1953, however true investigative journalism had given way to inaccurate sensationalism.

Sunday Dispatch

152nd Year. No. 7,889. 2½d. JANUARY 18, 1953. Radio Page 6

£500,000 Wasted On Three Useless Engines

RAILWAYS' BIGGEST FIASCO

They Tried To Hush It Up

By Sunday Dispatch Reporter

THREE huge railway engines, which cost altogether about £500,000 to build, now lie rusting and useless in sheds and sidings—silent and hidden evidence of the biggest fiasco produced by Britain's nationalised railways.

One of the Leader class locomotives.

This situation comes to light as the result of *Sunday Dispatch* inquiries, prompted by the threatened increase in fares and allegations of mismanagement on the railways.

The engines, 67ft.-long monsters of the Leader class, with driving cabins at each end, were built in 1948 and 1949 to "revolutionise" rail travel.

They were part of a £500,000 experiment undertaken by Mr. O. V. Bulleid, chief mechanical engineer of British Railways, Southern Region.

I can reveal that the region's officials regard the experiment as one of their biggest failures.

It was a failure that had been hushed up.

From the start the plan to build Mr. Bulleid's dream loco was kept secret.

But news leaked out late in 1948, when the designer gave the British Association some details of "a revolutionary steam locomotive."

The first of the Leaders, known to railwaymen as No. 36001, was then being built at the Southern Region works in Brighton. It started its trials in 1949, and was begun immediately on the other two.

Towed Back

From start to finish, the "revolutionary" gave trouble. Workers at the Eastleigh (Hants) sheds frequently saw No. 36001 being towed back for repair by an old-fashioned engine.

Firemen who worked aboard her during the test period reported the Leader was the most uncomfortable loco on the track.

Ventilation in the centre portion, where they stoked in a corridor running between the two driving cabins, was very poor.

One worker told me: "We knew the three Leaders as 'White Elephants.' Some were ridden in them used more lurid descriptions."

"Frequently the 'Flying Tramcar,' as others called her, broke down."

Two In One

Women In Prison

GODFREY WINN'S GREATEST SERIES

By The Editor Of The SUNDAY DISPATCH

FOR one hour yesterday, I sat enthralled as Godfrey Winn told me about one of the most remarkable experiences he has ever had in all his crowded, colourful life. He had just spent an entire day—from early morning to late at night—in Britain's most famous prison for women—Holloway.

He had talked to the prisoners, eaten their kind of meals, saw how they lived, how they dressed, where they slept. He talked over their problems with them and with the Governor and other officials of Holloway. Even the mothers whose babies were born during their sentence talked frankly and freely to Godfrey Winn.

HE WAS ABLE TO SEE AND DO ALL THIS BECAUSE HE HAS BEEN GIVEN A PRIVILEGE RARELY, IF EVER, GRANTED TO A WRITER—OFFICIAL PERMISSION TO VISIT EVERY TYPE OF WOMEN'S PRISON IN GREAT BRITAIN IN ORDER TO FIND OUT FOR HIMSELF THE TRUTH ABOUT THE CONDITION AND LIFE OF THE WOMEN WHO ARE KEPT IN BRITAIN'S JAILS.

Many sensational, highly coloured stories have been written about women's prisons, but Godfrey Winn's report will give the world the plain, uncoloured truth.

It is more gripping than any fanciful account could be.

The facts he has gathered in the course of his investigation will interest every reader of the SUNDAY DISPATCH as much as they interested me.

'ARISTOCRACY DOOMED AND DAMNED'

Shinwell Outburst Over The Coronation Plans

A FORMER Socialist Minister of Defence and Secretary of State for War, Mr. Emanuel Shinwell, yesterday attacked Coronation arrangements.

He said, at Halesowen, Worcestershire, that he had the highest respect for the young Queen and wished her long life and a successful reign. But when he read that the standard-bearers at the Coronation were all from the aristocracy, and particularly from the military, he wondered at it all.

We were in a democratic age and wanted this age to usher in an era of peace.

What more appropriate than that the Queen should be accompanied by her friends and by those who represented the scientific world, the medical profession, the nurses, miners, farm-workers, steel-workers, the railwaymen.

They were the salt of the earth.

FARES-RISE NOW MAY BE QUERIED AT WESTMINSTER

Police A To Fre On Theft

A MAN who had sworn he w crime for which he had was released from prison tion to get his bail reduced.

"Information has come to earlier, would have resulted in t detective sergeant told the W

ALARM OVER 'LOST' MAILBAG THAT WASN'T LOST AFTER ALL

By Sunday Dispatch Reporter

THE Mystery of the Missing Mailbag of Reading Station was solved late last night.

But only after detectives and G.P.O. officials had

Extract from the *Sunday Dispatch* newspaper.

Boiler and firebox from No. 36001 after removal for scrap. The firebox ribs are clearly visible with the side sheets partly cut through and ready for removal. The evidence of heat distortion is quite remarkable.

Collection of B. Curl

The next day the *Daily Telegraph* printed a more accurate assessment but its circulation was unlikely to reach the same numbers of the populace as the sunday newspaper. The damage had been done, and BR were now on the defensive and with any reference to Leader ignored whenever possible.

Meanwhile over in Ireland Bulleid astonished his critics by saying, '. . . . we will probably do something of the sort over here', but by now the news value of the project had dimmed and few heard such comments. Those in the know however were well aware that this was a further reference to the 'Turf Burner', one may perhaps only wonder about the thoughts of the Irish Railway officials!

Subsequently little reference was made to 'Leader' for some years. However, despite the actual locomotive having ceased to exist, aspects of its design were to be resurrected, ironically by the very group that had condemned it, BR.

The pivotless bogie for example appeared under 'Leader', then the three Southern main line diesels and finally the first generation of main line diesel-electrics, Class 40, 45 & 46. Similarly in 1967 the dashpot damping system was used by the Southern Region for its 90 mph electric sets on the Bournemouth Electrification scheme. These were in both cases a direct descendant of 'Leader' principles, but not referred to by BR as such.

Regretfully little else of the design found a place in future developments, the superb steam raising capacity of the boiler, the full weight available for adhesion, the symmetrical and continually even drive, none were used in the final progression of steam. Neither it would seem were any of Bulleid's ideas used for further progression in steam engine design.

So was it all a waste, in terms of time, effort and finance? With regard purely to cost the answer must be in the affirmative but with regard to other areas there is no clear cut answer.

Certainly Bulleid had tried to point the way forward. The problem really comes down to a matter of timing and, in this respect, the onset of nationalisation meant that No. 36001 was really condemned before she ever turned a wheel. It would have required a faultless performance from the outset to alter this. In the form No. 36001 took, the timing of her birth would never have been right, she was a hybrid and in essence stillborn.

But why such controversy over what was really a relatively small amount of money? Especially when the chapters of history are littered with similar engineering feats, TSR2, the on–off progress of the Channel Tunnel and more recently the Advanced Passenger Train. If we learn from the experience of others then the concept of these projects is not lost; if not we too are the losers. The time was never right for 'Leader', CC1, the 'Irish Turf Burner' came nearer to the ideal but still failed to perform exactly as needed and anyway by then it was already too late. Could it be that we failed 'Leader', rather than it failed us?

TEST OF 17 OCTOBER 1950

Place	Time		Pressure		Cut off %	Water in glass (F= 6½)	S'box vac. (in. of water)	Temp °F		Remarks
	Bkd. p.m.	Actual p.m.	Boiler	Stm. ch.				lge. tubes	small tubes	
Eastleigh	6.45	6.45	260	145	67	Full				
				140	15					
Allbrook		6.51¼	250	200	30	Full	4½	620	600	Engine worked very
			260	230	..		8	700	630	lightly to
			245	..	15		6½	..	..	Allbrook Jc
Shawford		6.57	240	..	18	5in.	8	..	640	and mainly
Shawford Jc.			225	220	..		8	710	635	due to this
St. Cross Tunnel			..	..	..		8½	..	..	5 min. lost to Winchester Jc.
Winchester		7.1¼	230	225	20	4in.	9	740	680	Showers of sparks from
Winchester Jc.	6.59	7.4	..	220	..	2½in.	..	750	700	chimney about 20%
			235	225			9	760	730	being alight on reaching ground. 15 mph PWS
Wallers Ash Box			250	240	20	2½in.	4	660	620	
Weston Box			240	235	..	2in.	7	720	680	
Micheldever		7.14½	220	205	..	2in.	8	720	685	B.P. & Water in glass
Litchfield Tunnel			185	160	..	2in.	6	715	675	not maintained
Worting Jc	7.19	7.23	200	60	..	2½in.				
Basingstoke	7.24	7.27	6 minutes taken to get engine set for taking water							
	7.32	7.32	260	130	67	2in.				
			255	160	15		4	630	580	
Hook		7.46½	240	135	..	1½in.	5	670	630	
Winchfield		7.49	230	120	..	1¼in.	4	665	625	
Fleet		7.55¼	230	120	..	1¼in.	5	650	610	
Farnboro'		7.55¼	230	120	..	1¾	..	645	600	
Brockwood		8.1	210	200	..					
Woking	8.5	8.3¼								To local line Sig. checks

TEST OF 2 NOVEMBER 1950

Place	Time		Pressure		Cut Off	Water in glass	S'box vac.	Temp °F		Remarks
	Bkd. p.m.	Act. p.m.	Blr.	Stm. Ch.	(%)	(F = 6½)	(in. of water)	Lge. tubes	small tubes	
Eastleigh	6.40	6.40	260	240	67	F	1	500	500	Started without difficulty
			270	130	25	"	1¾	600	585	
Allbrook Jc.	6.45	6.45½	245	240	10	"	2½	650	620	Pricker & dart used
			260	255	18	"	4	680	630	
Shawford		6.53½	230	225	"	"	6½	730	680	
Shawford			220	210	"	"	7	730	660	Pricker used
St. Cross Tunnel			"	"	"	"	"	"	"	
Winchester		6.58¾	245	240	"	"	9	750	700	" "
Winchester Jc.	6.59	7.1¾	255	225	"	"	10½	760	710	
Wallers Ash Box		7.5	245	220	"	"	"	750	700	Pricker & dart used
Weston Box		7.7	240	225	"	"	10	"	720	" "
Micheldever		7.9½	250	235	"	5½in.	"	785	750	
			260	250	20	5in.	13½	800	780	
Lichfield Tunnel		7.12½	255	240	"	4in.	"	820	800	
Worting Jc.	7.19	7.18½								Pricker used.
Basingstoke	7.24	7.26								Sig. stop 1½ min.

		17 October 1950	2 November 1950
Load (tons)		430	480
Coal			
(total) (cwt)		52½	22 (Eastleigh–Basingstoke only)
	lbs/mile	59.6	–
	llbs/mile (Eastleigh–Basingstoke only)	86.0	94.8
	lbs/D.B.h.p. hr*	6.5	6.4
	lbs/sq. ft. grate/hr (Eastleigh–Basingstoke only)	125	130
Water			
(total) gall		3570	1834 (Eastleigh–Basingstoke only)
	gall/mile	37.4	–
	gall/mile (Eastleigh–Basingstoke only)	55.0	70.5
	lbs/D.B.h.p. hr*	41.0	51.0
	lbs/hr (Eastleigh–Basingstoke only)	19,000	24,500

* Figures for 17 October refer to the complete trip Eastleigh to Woking and return. Figures for 2 November have been assessed from these on the basis of comparative coal and water figures for Eastleigh–Basingstoke.

APPENDIX A

THE PAGET LOCOMOTIVE

Sir Cecil Paget was Works Manager at Derby on the Midland Railway during the period 1904–1909. During this time he designed a 2-6-2 tender engine of larger dimensions than many of the machines then running on the MR with the intention of avoiding much of the double heading then necessary.

Externally there was much that was in keeping with the aesthetic Midland style, but within the engine there were incorporated eight single acting cylinders 18in. x 12in. stroke and with steam distribution by sleeve valves.

Paget's reasons for the use of sleeve valves were believed to come from the time he was an engineering student and in addition the success of a similar stationary engine installed in the power house at Derby Works.

The only known photograph of the Paget engine, with its origins in contemporary Midland design very apparent. What Paget and Bulleid failed to realise was that a sleeve valve engine would only work well when run at a constant speed. Most successful sleeve valve engines adopted this principle. The same principle occurred with dry firebox sides, they were ideal on a stationary machine but subjected to the vibration of a railway environment it was impossible to keep the bricks in position. Ironically another parallel was when it came to photographing the engine, for any attempt to do so whilst the Paget engine was at Derby was prohibited. Years later when 'Leader' was at Eastleigh a railway employee found photographing the machine had his film destroyed.

British Railways

The design also incorporated a dry back firebox with semicircular water jacket on top. The curved sides of the firebox were lined with firebricks of varying thickness. For this reason the firebox was wider than normal and in consequence the design was itself changed from a 4-6-0 to a 2-6-2 to provide for a greater space.

Reputedly the engine ran well and attained a speed in excess of 80 mph. In addition it seemed suitable for almost any type of duty.

Unfortunately, the politics within the Midland Railway were against the design regardless of any promise it showed, and with Paget himself removed from the position of Works Manager to Superintendant of the Traffic Department he was unable to continue with what was in reality a private design. Much of this was also because he could not provide sufficient private funds and the MR would not assist sufficiently.

Failures did occur, with both the lining of the firebox dry sides and also with the valve gear which was difficult to keep steam tight and free of seizure. When problems arose on the road the delays to other traffic did nothing to assist Paget's cause.

Given the number 2299, the engine ran trials to various destinations including Leicester. By 1913 it was in store at Derby and covered over by a sheet in the paint shop. It was scrapped in 1915.

Probably the best account of this machine was published in a booklet produced by the *Railway Gazette* in 1945 and can now be obtained to order at most libraries.

APPENDIX B

SOUTHERN RAILWAY AND SOUTHERN REGION LOCOMOTIVE STOCK

New and Withdrawn 1941–1951

	New	Withdrawn
Year ending		
31.12.41	6 MN	1
21.12.42	4 MN 40 Q1	2
21.12.43		9
21.12.44	2 MN	22
21.12.45	8 MN 20 WC	5
21.12.46	32 WC	24
21.12.47	19 WC 14 USA	44
21.12.48	8 MN 19 WC	71
21.12.49	2 MN 11 WC	90
21.12.50	9 WC	48
21.12.51	1 WC	204
Totals	194 additions	520 withdrawals

Nos. 36001–5 are not included in the above totals.

Locomotives on loan are also not included. In 1947 there were 30 Ministry of Supply 2-8-0 engines on the SR.

Engines withdrawn include members of the A12, K10, Paddlebox, F1, B1, B4, B4X, J, T1, Atlantics and large wheeled 0-6-2T classes.

During the war years few engines had been condemned. The years immediately afterwards involved condemnation of types overdue for withdrawal.

Commencing in 1951 there was a mass withdrawal of the smaller 4-4-0 classes, particulary as the influx of LMS tank engines and BR Standard types began to take effect. Both these types are not shown in the new totals.

APPENDIX C

Extracts from *Modern Transport* 26.10.47. 'New Conception of Steam Locomotive Design – Lessons for the Immediate future'.

O.V. Bulleid

'In the early days of railways the locomotives were purchased from outside builders and the railway company was content to operate them and allow them to be maintained by the builder . . . . In order that the repairs could be done economically the necessary machine tools and other equipment were provided gradually and it was soon appreciated that this equipment was equally suited in manufacturing new locomotives.

. . . . it will inevitably be suggested that the accepted methods of design or construction cannot be expected to give substantially better results. That is to say, the results were as good as could be expected with the designs, materials, finish, and methods of operation which were used. Consequently if we are to reach the higher level of achievement in continuity of service, which is now required, a new conception of the steam locomotive is also needed.

Such thoughts caused us to question the accepted ideas and forced us to investigate the locomotive as regards, (1) design, (2) use and (3) servicing. The very age of the steam locomtive has acted against its further development for its bad features have come to be accepted as inherent and inevitable. It is these bad features which enable other forms of transport to compete with it and consequently such features must be eliminated if the steam locomotive is to survive. Our investigations soon satisfied us there that was room for improvement under all three heads . . . .

. . . . What sort of locomotive may we expect to see if it is to meet the majority of our future requirements? . . . . The locomotive should be built (1) to be run over the majority of the company lines; (2) to be capable of working all classes of train up to 90 mph; (3) to have its whole weight available for braking and the highest percentage thereof for adhesion; (4) to be equally suited for running in both directions without turning with unobstructed look-out; (5) to be ready for service at short notice; (6) to be almost continually available; (7) to be suited for complete 'common use'; (8) to run not less than 100,000 miles between general overhauls with little or no attention at the running sheds; (9) to cause minimum wear and tear to the track; and (10) to use substantially less fuel and water per drawbar horsepower developed. . . .

. . . A new type of Southern engine has been designed, the construction of five has been authorised. The engine will incorporate the following features and it is hoped will satisfy the design criteria given above. The locomotive is carried on two six wheeled bogies, the general design of which follows that of the bogies I designed for use under the company's electric locomotives. . . . The engine develops a torque the uniformity of which is comparable with that of a nose suspended electric traction motor but has a higher speed range and the unsprung weight is less. The capacity of the boiler has been made greater, relative to the cylinder horsepower than in the case of any previous Southern locomotive. The cabs at the ends will give an improved lookout.

The engines are intended for working fast passenger trains of 480 tons weight over the difficult Southern Railway main line, and goods and mineral trains of up to 1200 tons; that is to say, something above the heaviest trains that would be required on the system. They carry sufficient fuel for 200 miles. . . .

APPENDIX D

COMPARATIVE TESTS WITH SOUTHERN REGION LOCOMOTIVES

Summary showing comparative performance based on Average results obtained.

EASTLEIGH – WOKING

	Engine No. 31630 'U' Class	Engine No. 36001 'Leader Class'	% Difference Class 'U' = 100%
Boiler pressure (lbs/in.)	187	240	28.3% greater
Steam Chest pressure (lbs/in.)	167	135	19.2% less
Exhaust pressure (lbs/in.)	1.81	7.3/6.0	–
Smokebox vacuum (in. water)	2.34	4.00	71% greater
Inlet Steam Temp. °F	478	546/564	–
Exhaust Steam Temp °F	220	285	29.5%
Smokebox A Steam Temp °F	570	574	0.7%
Smokebox B Steam Temp °F	578	620	7.26%
Trip			–
Coal lbs	1455	2457	68.8%
lbs/mile	29.75	50.17	68.7%
lbs/ton mile (incl engine)	0.0818	0.121	48.0%
lbs/hr (running time)	1125	1830	62.7%
lbs/sq. ft. grate/hr	45	71.8	59.6%
lbs/ D.B.H.P. hr	4.01	6.727	67.6%
Water gall	1245	1850	48.6%
gall/mile	25.44	37.78	48.5%
lbs/hr (running time)	9621	13790	43.3%
lbs/D.B.H.P. hr	34.34	50.66	47.5%
lbs/sq. ft. evap heating surface/hr	6.334	5.777	8.8% less
lbs/ton mile (incl. engine)	0.702	0.912	30.0% greater
Evaporation lbs. water/lb coal	8.554	7.532	12.0% less
Boiler Efficiency %	78.29	71.22	9.0% less
B. Th U's/D.B.H.P. hr	53893	90262	67.5% greater
Overall Efficiency %	4.72	2.82	40.25% less

APPENDIX E

COSTS OF LEADER PROJECT

	No. 36001			Repairs/ Maintenance No. 36001			Locos Nos. 36002–5			Totals		
	£	s.	d.	£	s.	d.	£	s.	d.	£	s.	d.
Materials	14,144	5	11	2064	14	8	61,478	9	0	77,687	9	7
Wages	14,295	14	1	2644	13	2	37,775	6	2	54,715	13	5
Workshop expenses	10,913	17	4	1621	13	10	28,651	7	0	41,186	18	2
Sup'tendance	1429	11	5	96	16	5	3748	16	0	5275	3	10
Totals	40,783	8	9	6427	18	1	131,653	18	2	178,865	5	0

Figures taken from Riddles reports of March and November 1950.

APPENDIX F

Memorandum by Mr. Bulleid 8.3.1950.

'As I was not satisfied that the axle loadings of the Leader sent to Mr. Riddles were correct I weighed No. 1 bogie at Brighton on 24.2.1950 . . .

The engine was weighed with the boiler full of cold water and with 1000 gallons of water in its tanks and 1¼ tons of coal.

. . . It is most desirable the spring chambers in the bogie frames be throughly cleaned out, all rust removed and the interiors painted with a good paint impervious to oil. When attention has been given to these points the engine should be rewheeled and reweighed and the springs readjusted. The engine should then resume its trial running.

The earlier anxieties in connection with the Leader were about the sleeve valves and the brick lining of the firebox.

Although it is unreasonable to expect such a major innovation as a sleeve valve engine to require no development (piston valves took many years to bring them even to their present state), the difficulty experienced through the breakage of the driving wings has been overcome.

The fire brick lining now fitted follows that of oil burning locomotives on which it has given very satisfactory results under more severe conditions. This lining should now give little, if any, trouble.

Other teething troubles may arise and to ascertain what they are, if any, it is essential the locomotive be put back on to the road.

The experience we have had with the engine so far indicates directions in which improvements can be made at a later date, i.e. when proceeding with the building of the remainder of the order.

I am quite satisfied the engine can be made a useful and valuable locomotive and Mr. Granshaw, the Locomotive Manager at Brighton, with the help he is receiving from Mr. Jarvis, the Chief Draughtsman, can be relied upon to see this is done.

I have not referred to the differences in weights between the two sides of the engine. If considered essential this difference can be removed at any time by reducing the water tank on No. 2 bogie on the right hand side by the width of the corridor, by removing the tanks on No. 1 bogie and by providing a new tank on No. 1 bogie ahead of the smokebox. This would improve the weight distribution as between the bogies. I do not consider this work need be done at this stage.

I shall always appreciate deeply having been permitted to follow the development of the Leader engine so far, as it has given me much valuable information for future work.

I would like to add my acknowledgement of the help I have had from everyone concerned and especially the courtesy I have always had from Mr. Riddles.

As I do not think my services are necessary any longer and as I feel I may well be an embarrassment, I shall be oblidged if I can be released from the arrangement made last September. I shall be available for consultation if desired and if I can be of help at any time I shall always be only too pleased to give it.'

(Signed) O.V. Bulleid.

APPENDIX G

Comments on Mr. Bulleid's Memorandum by R.A. Riddles. 24.3.1950.

'The locomotive has been weighed on a number of occasions both at Brighton and Eastleigh.

. . . .It must be stated that the locomotive as at present constructed is not suitable for unrestricted running at the high speeds for which it was designed. The design of the bogies in association with the unusual form of pedestal hornblocks and the particular type of roller bearing axleboxes used is not satisfactory and modifications will be needed if further trial running and dynamometer car tests which will be carried out are sufficiently promising to render this course justifiable.

The sleeve valves with which the six cylinders of this locomotive are fitted represent a major innovation and the need for more development work could reasonably be anticipated. The mechanism driving the valves, as orginally designed, allowed for the usual reciprocating motion combined with a limited amount of rotation of the sleeve valves to distribute the lubricant and equalise wear. Seizure of the sleeve valves has occurred on a number of occasions resulting in broken valves and valve rods . . . .

The mechanisim for imparting the rotational movement to the valves has now been removed, thus eliminating a source of weakness. Insufficinet mileage has since been run to say whether a permanent cure for the failures has been effected.

With the special design of boiler fitted to this locomotive, the inner firebox is not surrounded by water in accordance with normal practice. The firebox sides are built in firebrick supported on steel casing plates. The brick lining has been found to deteriorate very rapidly and in an attempt to overcome the trouble a much thicker lining has recently been fitted. The conditions which the firebox lining of this locomotive are required to withstand are fundamentally different from those existing with oil fired locomotives of conventional design. This lining has not yet been tried in service and it is not possible to say whether it will be free from trouble and have a reasonable life.

The thicker firebrick lining has the effect of reducing the grate area from 43.3 sq.ft. as originally designed, to 25.5 sq.ft., which will reduce the steaming capacity of the locomotive and tend seriously to increase coal consumption at a given rate of working.

. . . . A decision as to whether the remaining four locomotives should be completed must wait the results of further trial runs and dynamometer car tests which will be carried out.

I am not yet satisfied that the expenditure probably necessary to develop the locomotive into a useful and valuable unit will be justified.

A decision on this matter must await results of further trial running and dynamometer car tests. The facts will speak for themsleves in due course.

The weight on the two sides must certainly be equalised before the locomotive can be allowed to run in normal service at the speeds for which it has been designed.'

APPENDIX H

Extracts from R.C. Riddles memorandum to the Railway Executive 20.11.1950.

'In accordance with the terms of R.E. Memo M.2.880 the following further memorandum on the Leader locomotive is submitted.

Since my report dated 24.3.1950 was submitted, further trail runs have been made, including two series of dynamometer car tests to determine the performance of this locomotive in comparison with a conventional locomotive of comparable power characteristics.

. . . It was originally hoped, that adjustment to the axlebox pedestals and slides would improve the weight distribution, but it is now evident that extensive redesign of the locomotive would be necessary in order to obtain a distribution which could be considered satisfactory for running in normal service.

It was therefore necessary in order that further trials might be run, to overcome the unsatisfactory weight distribution temporarily by the addition of 5¼ tons of ballast located on the locomotive in such a way as to produce a more uniform distribution of weight between the left and right sides . . . . .

Renewed running of the locomotive revealed a number of minor defects, which culminated on 29th. June after a total mileage of only 6103, in the crank axle of No. 1 bogie fracturing and breaking in two pieces. Examination of the crank axle of No. 2 bogie revealed a number of small fatigue cracks and this axle would ultimately have failed in similar manner.

. . . The locomotive had to be sent into the Works and new driving wheels and crank axles were fitted on both bogies. With the locomotive as at present built it is very probable that these replaced axles would also fail.

. . . In view of the very high coal and water consumption, it was suspected that steam leakage was occuring and the pistons, sleeve valves and rings, were renewed and examined. Evidence of leakage was apparent and a number of new sleeve rings were fitted and all rings on pistons and valves were renewed . . . .Such a marked deterioration in performance for a locomotive after only approximately 6000 miles is exceptional and the trials have indicated that, with the present design, this rapid deterioration could only be corrected by frequently stopping the locomotive for examination and repairs to the valves and pistons . . . . compared with that of modern main line locomotives of more conventional design where the valves and pistons are normally only examined at intervals of 20–36000 miles . . .

. . . In the course of the trials attention was given to the operating conditions as far as the engine crews are concerned . . . . Men have complained of the high temperature in the firemans cab . . . .the firemans position becomes intolerable if attempts are made to run the engine chimney first, owing to the very hot air which emerges from the corridor when running in this direction. With the present arrangement one of the aims of the locomotive is thus defeated and it would be necessary for turning to take place at the end of each journey.

. . . There are only two alternatives which now present themselves in respect of the future of this class of locomotive. They are;

(a) To make a number of major modifications to the present design with a view to overcoming the difficulties which have been experienced and the difficulties which have been revealed;
or

(b) To scrap the locomotive so far completed and the other four in varying stages of construction.

The former course would involve the following in respect of the matters referred to above;–

(1) The high coal and water consumption is due, to a large extent, to steam leakage past the sleeve valves, pistons and rings. It is also due to the high rate of combustion made necessary by the reduction in grate area, resulting from the thicker firebrick walls which experience shows to be essential.

To correct these deficiencies would, in my opinion, involve a major redesign of the cylinders, eliminating the sleeve valves and replacing them with piston valves . . .

(2) To reduce the total weight of the locomotive by 20 tons, thus bringing it into conformity with the original diagram . . . . would be virtually impossible . . .

(3). . . . At present the boiler is offset from the longitudinal centre line of the locomotive. The weight distribution could be corrected only by placing the boiler on the centre line, which would involve major alterations to the design of the locomotive or by a complete redistribution of the water tanks which also would involve extensive modifications.

In either case it is doubtful whether the present access which exists between the drivers cab and fireman could be retained. This would involve an automatic device in the drivers cab on similar principle to a 'dead-mans' handle on electric stock, (which would be an undesirable though essential complication) or three men would always be required on the locomotive when on the main line.

(4) The present axlebox assembly would require to be completely redesigned to give sufficient freedom to ensure the safety of the locomotive as a vehicle on the track, and to provide the necessary flexibility to eliminate breakage of the crank axle.

It is not possible to say at this stage whether such redesign might not involve the elimination of the chains connecting the coupled axles and their replacement by coupling rods.

(5) It is diffcicult at this stage to suggest anything that could be done to ensure tolerable conditions for the fireman . . .

(6) The defects which are known to exist in the welding of part of the boiler of this locomotive would require to be rectified. Part of the welding of the boiler in the completed locomotive was subjected to X-Ray examination . . . The completed boilers for the other four locomotives, however were not subject to any kind of X-Ray examination and I should not be prepared to allow them to go out into service until this precaution has been duly carried out.

Expenditure amounting to £178,865 has already been incurred. So far it has not been possible, nor will it be possible, to place the locomotive in revenue earning service without further heavy expense. I have not estimated what this further expense might be because, even were it incurred and all the defects eliminated the locomotive, as modified, would offer no advantages compared with one of the conventional well-tried design.

I am compelled therefore to RECOMMEND that the second alternative namely, the completed Locomotive and the other four in various stages of construction, should be scrapped . . . .

(Sgd) R.A. Riddles.

APPENDIX I

The Turf Burner

Following his resignation from the position of C.M.E. of the SR, Bulleid accepted a similar post on the C.I.E. in Ireland.

Almost at once he commenced work on a further novel steam design, officially referred to as 'CC1' and known publicly as the 'Turf Burner'. In many respects the principles of the locomotive followed those previously incorporated in the 'Leader' design and included a machine with total adhesion carried on two powered bogies.

A preliminary start also involved the conversion of an existing steam locomtive to burn peat, for as a country Ireland possessed no natural coal deposits and so the opportunity was taken to take advantage of what local fuel existed.

Following a satisfactory start CC1 took shape at the Inchicore Works. The bogies each incorporated two cylinders this time actuated by piston valves, the final drive was again by chain.

Plans exist for a possible conversion of the engine to oil burning but this was never carried out. Even so there were a number of futuristic principles including a fan assisted draught.

The first outing on the main line was in October 1957 and although several quite successful tests were undertaken the engine never worked a public passenger train although it did operate a number of goods services.

Unfortunately for the engine, Bulleid had retired from Ireland in May 1958 and with him went the impetus for the design. By this time as well there was pressure to convert the system to diesel operation and so after a period in store at Inchicore Works the engine was finally scrapped in 1965.

A full description of the machine is available in *The Turf Burner – Ireland's Last Steam Design* by J.W.P. Rowledge, published by the Irish Railway Record Society.

BIBLIOGRAPHY

Bulleid Last Giant of Steam, Sean Day Lewis, George Allen & Unwin.
Bulleid of the Southern, p. 129, H.A.V. Bulleid, Ian Allen.
Bulleid's Locomotives Brian Haresnape, Ian Allen.
Locomotive Panorama, E.S. Cox, Ian Allen.
Master Builders of Steam, H.A.V. Bulleid, Ian Allen.
The Turf Burner – Ireland's Last Steam Locomotive Design, J.W.P. Rowledge, Irish Railway Record Society.
Chapelon – Genius of French Steam, Col. H.C.B. Rogers, Ian Allen.

Also reports from various issues of:
Engineering
Journal of Locomotive Engineers
Journal of the Stephenson Locomotive Society
Locomotive Railway Carriage and Wagon Review
Mechanical Engineering
Modern Transport
Railway Executive reports on the tests of the 'Leader' Class Locomotive.
Railway Magazine
Railway World
Steam World
The Locomotive
The Railway Gazette
Trains Illustrated

INDEX